THE THIRD BOOK OF
AFTER MIDNIGHT STORIES

Brian Lumley   Alma Priestley
R. Chetwynd-Hayes   A.L. Barker   J.C. Trewin
John Whitbourn   Jean Stubbs   Ross McKay
Mike Sims   Derek Stanford   Meg Buxton
John Marsh   Kelvin I. Jones
Fred Urquhart   Lanyon Jones

In the same series

After Midnight Stories
The Second Book of After Midnight Stories

THE THIRD BOOK OF
After Midnight Stories

A Kimber Ghost Book

Edited by
AMY MYERS

WILLIAM KIMBER · LONDON

First published in 1987 by
WILLIAM KIMBER & CO. LIMITED
100 Jermyn Street, London SW1Y 6EE

© Brian Lumley, 1987
© Alma Priestley, 1987
© R. Chetwynd-Hayes, 1987
© A.L. Barker, 1987
© J.C. Trewin, 1987
© John Whitbourn, 1987
© Jean Stubbs, 1975
© Ross McKay, 1987
© Mike Sims, 1987
© Derek Stanford, 1987
© Meg Buxton, 1987
© John Marsh, 1987
© Kelvin I. Jones, 1987
© Fred Urquhart, 1987
© Lanyon Jones, 1987

ISBN 0-7183-0667-8

This book is copyright. No part of it may be reproduced in any form without permission in writing from the publishers except by a reviewer who wishes to quote brief passages in a review written for inclusion in a newspaper, magazine, radio or television broadcast.

Photoset in North Wales by
Derek Doyle & Associates Mold, Clwyd
and printed in Great Britain by
Biddles Limited, Guildford and King's Lynn

Contents

	Acknowledgements	7
I	The Thin People *by Brian Lumley*	9
II	The Neapolitan Bedroom *by Alma Priestley*	22
III	Moving Day *by R. Chetwynd-Hayes*	40
IV	Element of Doubt *by A.L. Barker*	57
V	The Manse *by J.C. Trewin*	70
VI	Waiting for a Bus *by John Whitbourn*	84
VII	The Band in the Park *by Jean Stubbs*	93
VIII	The Indian's Grave *by Ross McKay*	110
IX	Warm as Snow *by Mike Sims*	118
X	Meeting Mr Singleton *by Derek Stanford*	129
XI	The Neighbours *by Meg Buxton*	140
XII	The Whisperer *by John Marsh*	154
XIII	Mandrake *by Kelvin I. Jones*	169
XIV	Swing High, Willie Brodie *by Fred Urquhart*	182
XV	The Nine Lessons and Carols *by Lanyon Jones*	198
	Notes on the Contributors	205

Acknowledgements

The publishers and editor would like to thank all those who have contributed to *The Third Book of After Midnight Stories* and make acknowledgement as follows: to the authors for 'The Neapolitan Bedroom', 'Moving Day', 'Element of Doubt', 'The Manse', 'Waiting for a Bus', 'The Indian's Grave', 'Warm as Snow', 'Meeting Mr Singleton', 'The Neighbours', 'The Whisperer', 'Mandrake', 'Swing High, Willie Brodie' and 'The Nine Lessons and Carols', to the author for 'The Band in the Park' which was first published in *The Eleventh Ghost Book* edited by Aidan Chambers, Barrie & Jenkins, 1975; and to the author and the Dorian Literary Agency for 'The Thin People'.

I

The Thin People
Brian Lumley

1

Funny place, Barrows Hill. Not *Barrow's* Hill, no. Barrows without the apostrophe. For instance: you won't find it on any map. You'll find maps whose borders approach it, whose corners impinge, however slightly, upon it, but in general it seems that cartographers avoid it. It's too far out from the centre for the tubes, hasn't got a main-line station, has lost much of its integrity by virtue of all the infernal demolition and reconstruction going on around and within it. But it's still there. Buses run to and from, and the older folk who live there still call it Barrows Hill.

When I went to live there in the late '70s I hated the place. There was a sense of senility, of inherent idiocy about it. A damp sort of place. Even under a hot summer sun, damp. You could feel blisters of fungus rising even under the freshest paint. Not that the place got painted very much. Not that I saw, anyway. No, for it was like somewhere out of Lovecraft: decaying, diseased, inbred.

Barrows Hill. I didn't stay long, a few months. Too long, really. It gave you the feeling that if you delayed, if you stood still for just one extra moment, then that it would grow up over you and you'd become a part of it. There are some old, old places in London, and I reckoned Barrows Hill was of the oldest. I also reckoned it for its *genius loci*; like it was a focal point for secret things. Or perhaps not a focal point, for that might suggest a radiation – a spreading outwards – and as I've said, Barrows Hill was ingrown. The last bastion of the strange old things of London. Things like the thin people. The very tall, very thin people.

Now nobody — but nobody *anywhere* — is ever going to believe me about the thin people, which is one of the two reasons I'm not afraid to tell this story. The other is that I don't live there anymore. But when I did ...

I suspect now, that quite a few people — ordinary people, that is — knew about them. They wouldn't admit it, that's all, and probably still won't. And since all of the ones who'd know live on Barrows Hill, I really can't say I blame 'em. There was one old lad lived there, however, who knew *and* talked about them. To me. Since he had a bit of a reputation (to be frank, they called him 'Balmy Bill of Barrows Hill') I didn't pay a deal of attention at first. I mean, who would?

Barrows Hill had a pub, a couple of pubs, but the one most frequented was 'The Railway'. A hangover from a time when there really was a railway, I supposed. A couple of years ago there had been another, a serious rival to 'The Railway' for a little while, when someone converted an old block into a fairly modern pub. But it didn't last. Whoever owned the place might have known something, but probably not. Or he wouldn't have been so stupid as to call his place 'The Thin Man'! It was only open for a week or two before burning down to the ground.

But that was before my time and the only reason I make mention of pubs, and particularly 'The Railway', is because that's where I met Balmy Bill. He was there because of his disease, alcoholism, and I was there because of mine, heartsickness — which, running at a high fever, showed all signs of mutating pretty soon into Bill's problem. In short, I was hitting the bottle.

Now this is all incidental information, of course, and I don't intend to go into it other than to say it was our problems brought us together. As unlikely a friendship as any you might imagine. But Balmy Bill was good at listening, and I was good at buying booze. And so we were good company.

One night, however, when I ran out of money, I made the mistake of inviting him back to my place. (My place — hah! A bed, a loo and a typewriter; a poky little place up some wooden stairs, like a penthouse kennel; oh, yes, and a bonus in the shape of a cupboard converted to a shower.) But I had a couple bottles of beer back there and a half-bottle of gin, and when I'd finished crying on Balmy Bill's shoulder it wouldn't be far for me to fall into bed. What did surprise me was how hard it was to get him back there. He started complaining the moment we left the bar – or rather, as soon as he saw which way we were headed.

'Up the Larches? You live up there, off Barchington Road? Yes, I remember you told me. Well, and maybe I'll just stay in the pub a while after all. I mean, if you live right up *there* – well, it's out of my way, isn't it?'

'Out of your way? It's a ten minute walk, that's all! I thought you were thirsty?'

'Thirsty I am – always! Balmy I'm not – they only say I am 'cos they're frightened to listen to me.'

'They?'

'People!' he snapped, sounding unaccustomedly sober. Then, as if to change the subject: 'A half-bottle of gin, you said?'

'That's right, Gordon's. But if you want to get back on down to "The Railway" ...'

'No, no, we're half-way there now,' he grumbled, hurrying along beside me, almost taking my arm in his nervousness. 'And anyway, it's a nice bright night tonight. They're not much for light nights.'

'They?' I asked again.

'People!' Despite his short, bowed legs, he was half a pace ahead of me. 'The thin people.' But where his first word had been a snarl, his last three were whispered, so that I almost missed them entirely.

Then we were up Larches Avenue – *the* Larches as Balmy Bill had it – and closing fast on twenty-two, and suddenly it was very quiet. Only the scrape of dry, blown leaves on the pavement. Autumn, and the trees half-naked. Moonlight falling through webs of high, black, brittle branches.

'Plenty of moon,' said Bill, his voice hushed. 'Thank God – in whom I really don't believe – for that. But *no street lights*! You see that? Bulbs all missing. That's them.'

'Them?' I caught his elbow, turning him into my gateway – if there'd been a gate. There wasn't, just the post, which served as my landmark whenever I'd had a skinful.

'Them, yes!' he snapped, staring at me as I turned my key in the lock. 'Damn young fool!'

And so up the creaky stairs to my little cave of solitude, and Balmy Bill shivering despite the closeness of the night and warmth of the place, which leeched a lot of its heat from the houses on both sides, and from the flat below, whose elderly lady occupier couldn't seem to live in anything other than an oven; and in through my own door, into the 'living' room, where Bill closed the curtains across the jutting bay windows as if he'd lived there all of his life. But not before he'd peered out into the night street, his eyes darting this way and that, round and bright in his lined, booze-desiccated face.

Balmy, yes. Well, maybe he was and maybe he wasn't. 'Gin,' I said, passing him the bottle and a glass. 'But go easy, yes? I like a nip myself, you know.'

'A nip? A nip? Huh! If I lived here I'd need more than a nip. This is the middle of it, this is. The very middle!'

'Oh?' I grinned. 'Myself, I had it figured for the living end!'

He paced the floor for a few moments – three paces there, three back – across the protesting boards of my tiny room, before pointing an almost accusing finger at me. 'Chirpy tonight, aren't you? Full of beans!'

'You think so?' Yes, he was right. I did feel a bit brighter. 'Maybe I'm over it, eh?'

He sat down beside me. 'I certainly hope so, you daft young sod! And now maybe you'll pay some attention to my warnings and get yourself a place well away from here.'

'Your warnings? Have you been warning me, then?' It dawned on me that he had, for several weeks, but I'd been too wrapped up in my own misery to pay him much heed. And who would? After all, he was Balmy Bill.

' 'Course I have!' he snapped. 'About them bloody –'

'– Thin people,' I finished it for him. 'Yes, I remember now.'

'Well?'

'Eh?'

'Are you or aren't you?'

'I'm listening, yes.'

'No, no, *no*! Are you or aren't you going to find yourself new lodgings?'

'When I can afford it, yes.'

'You're in danger here, you know. They don't like strangers. Strangers change things, and they're against that. They don't like anything strange, nothing new. They're a dying breed, I fancy, but while they're here they'll keep things the way they like 'em.'

'Okay,' I sighed. 'This time I really am listening. You want to start at the beginning?'

He answered my sigh with one of his own, shook his head impatiently. 'Daft young bugger! If I didn't like you I wouldn't bother. But all right, for your own good, one last time ... just listen and I'll tell you what I know. It's not much, but it's the last warning you'll get ...'

2

'Best thing ever happened for 'em must have been the lampposts, I reckon.'

'Dogs?' I raised my eyebrows.

He glared at me and jumped to his feet. 'Right, that's it, I'm off!'

'Oh, sit down, sit down!' I calmed him. 'Here, fill your glass again. And I promise I'll try not to interrupt.'

'Lampposts!' he snapped, his brows black as thunder. But he sat and took the drink. 'Yes, for they imitate them, see? And thin, they can hide behind them. Why, they can stand so still that on a dark night you wouldn't know the difference! Can you imagine that, eh? Hiding behind or imitating a lamppost!'

I tried to imagine it, but: 'Not really,' I had to admit. Now, however, my levity was becoming a bit forced. There was something about his intensity – the way his limbs shook in a manner other than alcoholic – which was getting through to me. 'Why should they hide?'

'Freaks! Wouldn't you hide? A handful of them, millions of us. We'd hound 'em out, kill 'em off!'

'So why don't we?'

' 'Cos we're all smart young buggers like you, that's why!

'Cos we don't *believe* in 'em.'

'But you do.'

Bill nodded, his three or four day growth of hair quivering on jowls and upper lip. 'Seen 'em,' he said, 'and seen ... *evidence* of them.'

'And they're real people? I mean, you know, human? Just like me and you, except ... thin?'

'And tall. Oh – *tall*!'

'Tall?' I frowned. 'Thin and tall. How tall? Not as tall as –'

'Lampposts,' he nodded, 'yes. Not during the day, mind you, only at night. At night they –' (he looked uncomfortable, as if it had suddenly dawned on him how crazy this all must sound) '– they sort of, well, kind of *unfold* themselves.'

I thought about it, nodded. 'They unfold themselves. Yes, I see.'

'No, you don't see,' his voice was flat, cold, angry now. 'But you will, if you hang around here long enough.'

'Where do they live,' I asked, 'these tall, thin people?'

'In thin houses,' he answered, matter-of-factly.

'Thin houses?'

'Sure! Are you telling me you haven't noticed the thin houses? Why, this place of yours very nearly qualifies! Thin houses, yes. Places where normal people wouldn't dream of setting up. There's half-a-dozen such in Barchington, and a couple right here in the Larches!' He shuddered and I bent to turn on an extra bar in my electric fire.

'Not cold, mate,' Bill told me then. 'Hell no! Enough booze in me to keep me warm. But I shudder every time I think of 'em. I mean, what *do* they do?'

'Where do they work, you mean?'

'Work?' he shook his head. 'No, they don't work. Probably do a bit of tea-leafing. Burglary, you know. Oh, they'd get in anywhere, the thin people. But what do they *do*?'

I shrugged.

'I mean, me and you, we watch telly, play cards, chase the birds, read the paper. But them ...'

It was on the tip of my tongue to suggest maybe they go into the woods and frighten owls, but suddenly I didn't feel half so flippant. 'You said you'd seen them?'

'Seen 'em sure enough, once or twice,' he confirmed. 'And

weird! One, I remember, came out of his thin house – thin house in Barchington, I could show you it sometime in daylight. Me, I was behind a hedge sleeping it off. Don't ask me how I got there, drunk as a lord! Anyway, something woke me up.

'Down at its bottom the hedge was thin where cats come through. It was night and the council men had been round during the day putting bulbs in the street lights, so the place was all lit up. And directly opposite, there's this thin house and its door slowly opening; and out comes this bloke into the night, half of him yellow from the lamplight and half black in shadow. See, right there in front of the thin house is a street lamp.

'But this chap looks normal enough, you know? A bit stiff in his movements: he sort of moves jerky, like them contortionists who hook their feet over their shoulders and walk on their hands. Anyway, he looks up and down the street, and he's obviously satisfied no one's there. Then –

'– He slips back a little into the shadows until he comes up against the wall of his house, and he – unfolds!

'I see the light glinting down one edge of him, see it suddenly split into two edges at the bottom, sort of hinged at the top. And the split widens until he stands in the dark there like a big pair of dividers. And then one half swings up until it forms a straight line, perpendicular – and now he's ten feet tall. Then the same again, only this time the division takes place in the middle. Like ... like a joiner's wooden three-foot ruler, with hinges so he can open it up, you know?'

I nodded, fascinated despite myself. 'And that's how they're built, eh? I mean, well, hinged?'

'Hell, no!' he snorted. 'You can fold your arms on their elbows, can't you? Or your legs on their knees? You can bend from the waist and touch your toes? Well I sure can! Their joints may be a little different from ours, that's all – maybe like the joints of certain insects. Or maybe not. I mean, their science is different from ours, too. Perhaps they fold and unfold themselves the same way they do it to other things – except it doesn't do them any harm. I dunno ...'

'What?' I asked, puzzled. 'What other things do they fold?'

'I'll get to that later,' he told me darkly, shivering. 'Where was I?'

'There he was,' I answered, 'all fifteen foot of him, standing in the shadows. Then –?'

'A car comes along the street, sudden like!' Bill grabbed my arm.

'Wow!' I jumped. 'He's in trouble, right?'

Balmy Bill shook his head. 'No way. The car's lights are on full, but that doesn't trouble the thin man. He's not stupid. The car goes by, lighting up the walls with its beam, and where the thin man stood in shadows against the wall of his thin house –'

'Yes?'

'A drainpipe, all black and shiny!'

I sat back. 'Pretty smart.'

'You better believe they're smart. Then, when it's dark again, out he steps. And *that's* something to see! Those giant strides – but quick, almost a flicker. Blink your eyes and he's moved – and between each movement his legs coming together as he pauses, and nothing to see but a pole. Up to the lamppost he goes, seems almost to melt into it, hides behind it. And *plink*! – out goes the light. After that ... in ten minutes he had the whole street black as night in a coalmine. And yours truly lying there in somebody's garden, scared and shivering and dying to throw up.'

'And that was it?'

Balmy Bill gulped, tossed back his gin and poured himself another. His eyes were huge now, skin white where it showed through his whiskers. 'God, no – that wasn't it – there was more! See, I figured later that I must have got myself drunk deliberately that time – so's to go up there and spy on 'em. Oh, I now that sounds crazy now, but you know what it's like when you're drunk mindless. Jesus, these days I can't *get* drunk! But these were early days I'm telling you about.'

'So what happened next?'

'Next – he's coming back down the street! I can hear him: *click*, pause ... *click*, pause ... *click*, pause, stilting it along the pavement – and I can see him in my mind's eye, doing his impression of a lamppost with every pause. And suddenly I get this feeling, and I sneak a look around. I mean, the frontage of this garden I'm in is so tiny, and the house behind me is –'

I saw it coming. 'Jesus!'

'A thin house,' he confirmed it, 'right!'

'So now *you* were in trouble.'

He shrugged, licked his lips, trembled a little. 'I was lucky, I suppose. I squeezed myself into the hedge, lay still as death. And *click*, pause ... *click*, pause, getting closer all the time. And then, behind me, for I'd turned my face away – the slow creaking as the door of the thin house swung open! And the second thin person coming out and, I imagine, unfolding him- or herself, and the two of 'em standing there for a moment, and me near dead of fright.'

'And?'

'*Click-click*, pause; *click-click*, pause; *click- click* – and away they go. God only knows where they went, or what they did, but me? – I gave 'em ten minutes' start and then got up, and ran, and stumbled, and forced my rubbery legs to carry me right out of there. And I haven't been back. Why, this is the closest I've been to Barchington since that night, and too close by far!'

I waited for a moment but he seemed done. Finally I nodded. 'Well, that's a good story, Bill, and –'

'I'm not finished!' he snapped. 'And it's not just a story ...'

'There's more?'

'Evidence,' he whispered. 'The evidence of your own clever-bugger eyes!'

I waited.

'Go to the window,' said Bill, 'and peep out through the curtains. Go on, do it.'

I did.

'See anything funny?'

I shook my head.

'Blind as a bat!' he snorted. 'Look at the street lights – or the absence of lights. I showed you once tonight. They've nicked all the bulbs.'

'Kids,' I shrugged. 'Hooligans. Vandals.'

'Huh!' Bill sneered. 'Hooligans, here? Unheard of, Vandals? You're joking! What's to vandalize? And when did you last see kids playing in these streets, eh?'

He was right. 'But a few missing light bulbs aren't hard evidence,' I said.

'All *right*!' he pushed his face close and wrinkled his nose at me. 'Hard evidence, then.' And he began to tell me the final part of his story ...

3

'Cars!' Balmy Bill snapped, in that abrupt way of his. 'They can't bear them. Can't say I blame 'em much, not on that one. I hate the noisy, dirty, clattering things myself. But tell me: have you noticed anything a bit queer – about cars, I mean – in these parts?'

I considered for a moment, replied: 'Not a hell of a lot of them.'

'Right!' He was pleased. 'On the rest of the Hill, nose to tail. Every street overflowing. 'Specially at night when people are in the pubs or watching the telly. But here? Round Barchington and the Larches and a couple of other streets in this neighbourhood? Not a one to be seen!'

'Not true,' I said. 'There are two cars in this very street. Right now. Look out the window and you should be able to see them.'

'Bollocks!' said Bill.

'Pardon?'

'Bollocks!' he gratefully repeated. 'Them's not *cars*! Rusting old bangers. Spoke-wheels and all. Twenty, thirty years they've been trundling about. The thin people are *used* to them. It's the big shiny new ones they don't like. And so, if you park your car up here overnight – trouble!'

'Trouble?' But here I was deliberately playing dumb. Here I knew what he meant well enough. I'd seen it for myself: the occasional shiny car, left overnight, standing there the next morning with its tyres slashed, windows smashed, lamps kicked in.

He could see it in my face. 'You know what I mean, all right. Listen, couple of years ago there was a flash Harry type from the city used to come up here. There was a barmaid he fancied in 'The Railway' – and she was taking all he could give her. Anyway, he was flash, you know? One of the gang lads and a rising star. And a flash car to go with it. Bullet-proof windows, hooded lamps, reinforced panels – the lot. Like a bloody tank, it was. But –' Bill sighed.

'He used to park it up here, right?'

He nodded. 'Thing was, you couldn't threaten him. You know what I mean? Some people you can threaten, some you shouldn't threaten, and some you mustn't. He was one you mustn't. Trouble is, so are the thin people.'

'So what happened?'

'When they slashed his tyres, he lobbed bricks through the windows. And he had a knowing way with him. He tossed 'em through thin house windows. Then one night he parked down on the corner of Barchington. Next morning – they'd drilled holes right through the plate, all over the car. After that – he didn't come back for a week or so. When he did come back ... well, he must've been pretty mad.'

'What did he do?'

'Threw something else – something that made a bang! A damn big one! You've seen that thin, derelict shell on the corner of Barchington? Oh, it was him, sure enough, and he got it right, too. A thin house. Anybody in there, they were goners. And *that* did it!'

'They got him?'

'They got his car! He parked up one night, went down to 'The Railway,' when the bar closed took his lady-love back to her place, and in the morning –'

'They'd wrecked it – his car, I mean.'

'Wrecked it? Oh, yes, they'd done that. They'd *folded* it!'

'Come again?'

'Folded it!' he snapped. 'Their funny science. Eighteen inches each way, it was. A cube of folded metal. No broken glass, no split seams, no splintered plastic. Folded all neat and tidy. An eighteen-inch cube.'

'They'd put it through a crusher, surely?' I was incredulous.

'Nope – folded.'

'Impossible!'

'Not to them. Their funny science.'

'So what did he do about it?'

'Eh? Do? He looked at it, and he thought, "What if I'd been

sitting *in* the bloody thing?" Do? He did what I would do, what you would do. He went away. We never did see him again.'

The half-bottle was empty. We reached for the beers. And after a long pull I said: 'You can kip here if you want, on the floor. I'll toss a blanket over you.'

'Thanks,' said Balmy Bill, 'but no thanks. When the beer's gone I'm gone. I wouldn't stay up here to save my soul. Besides, I've a bottle of my own back home.'

'Sly old sod!' I said.

'Daft young bugger!' he answered without malice. And twenty minutes later I let him out. Then I crossed to the windows and looked out at him, at the street all silver in moonlight.

He stood at the gate (where it should be) swaying a bit and waving up at me, saying his thanks and farewell. Then he started off down the street.

It was quiet out there, motionless. One of those nights when even the trees don't move. Everything frozen, despite the fact that it wasn't nearly cold. I watched Balmy Bill out of sight, craning my neck to see him go, and —

— Across the road, three lampposts — where there should only be two! The one on the left was okay, and the one to the far right. But the one in the middle? I never had seen that one before. I blinked bleary eyes, gasped, blinked again. Only *two* lampposts!

Stinking drunk — drunk as a skunk — utterly boggled!

I laughed as I tottered from the window, switched off the light, staggered into my bedroom. The balmy old bastard had really had me going. I'd really started to believe. And now the booze was making me see double — or something. Well, just as long as it was lampposts and not pink elephants! Or thin people! And I went to bed laughing.

... But I wasn't laughing the next morning.

Not after they found him, old Balmy Bill of Barrows Hill. Not after they called me to identify him.

'Their funny science,' he'd called it. The way they folded things. And Jesus, they'd folded him, too. Right down into an eighteen-inch cube. Ribs and bones and skin and muscles — the lot. Nothing broken, you understand, just folded. No blood or guts or anything nasty – nastier by far *because* there was nothing.

And they'd dumped him in a garbage-skip at the end of the street. The couple of local youths who found him weren't even sure what they'd found, until they spotted his face on one side of the cube. But I won't go into that ...

Well, I moved out of there just as soon as I could – do you blame me? – since when I've done a lot of thinking about it. Fact is, I haven't thought of much else.

And I suppose old Bill was right. At least I hope so. Things he'd told me earlier, when I was only half listening. About them being the last of their sort, and Barrows Hill being the place they've chosen to sort of fade away in, like a thin person's 'elephant's graveyard,' you know?

Anyway, there are no thin people here, and no thin houses. Vandals aplenty, and so many cars you can't count, but nothing out of the ordinary.

Lampposts, yes, and posts to hold up the telephone wires, of course. Lots of them. But they don't bother me anymore.

See, I know *exactly* how many lampposts there are. And I know exactly *where* they are, every last one of them. And God help the man ever plants a new one without telling me first!

II

The Neapolitan Bedroom

Alma Priestley

'Amazin',' said Trevor Bennett. 'The lift works. Is this a record?'

'Ssh –' Sandra put her finger to his lips. 'You don't need to say things like that here.' She leaned contentedly against him as the Graymeads lift moved them efficiently to the fourth floor and stopped without a creak. 'These aren't your vandalised council flats, Trevor. They're private, they're special – you can tell.'

'Special rent, all right, I can tell that.' Trevor was consulting numbers on doors. 'Must be this way, Sandra – come on.'

'Not as bad as we thought, though.' She was hurrying to keep up with his long strides. 'The rent, I mean – we can manage it.'

'Just.'

'And if it gets us out of that bedsitter – oh, I can't believe it – us with a whole flat!'

'Should never have bought that video, if you ask me. Should be savin' for a deposit on a house, not payin' out rents for a place like this. – Here we are, Sandra – Number 51. Must be a hell of a long way up.'

'Think of the view.' She felt for his hand and pressed it. 'I've got butterflies in me stomach, Trev. What do you think it'll be like?'

'Soon find out.' He pressed a bell marked Wilkins and grinned down at her small, fair, anxious face. 'What you worryin' about, then? It's only a flat. If we don't get this one, we'll get another.'

'But I want this one, I know I do.' Sandra rocked to and fro on her high heels. 'She's takin' for ever to come, isn't she? Do you think she's old?'

Mrs Wilkins was not old, only very heavily pregnant. She stood now in the doorway of the flat, waxen, fragile, in spite of her size, and stared at them with dark apprehensive eyes. It didn't seem as though she was expecting them.

Trevor said: 'Mrs Wilkins? We're the people who 'phoned about seein' the flat – name's Bennett.'

'It is all right to come in, isn't it?' asked Sandra, quickly. 'I mean, now? Trevor's got to be back at the Gas Board at two and I'm due at the shop at half past –'

'Oh, yes, of course –' Mrs Wilkins pushed her red-blonde hair from her brow with a freckled hand. 'Please – do come in – sorry about the mess – you know what it's like –'

What mess? The sittingroom, dominated by a large picture window, was as neat and impersonal as a hotel room, nothing out of place, no signs of life, a dead person's room – Oh, how stupid – of course, everything was packed – Mrs Wilkins said so – the boxes were in the spare room – she would be moving out tomorrow. Sandra gave a sigh of relief and walked about the room, hugging her plump arms, quietening the butterflies in her stomach, taking everything in.

'You goin' to a house?' asked Trevor, speaking in a low hushed voice as though to an invalid, as though he thought if he spoke in his normal tones Mrs Wilkins, in spite of her size, might just float away.

'Er – no.' She lumbered to a chair by the window and sat down. 'Just another flat. Across the city.'

'With a garden?' asked Sandra. 'For the baby?'

'No. No garden. Maybe later.' Mrs Wilkins lay back and closed her eyes, then sat up, blushing. 'Oh, I'm sorry. I don't know what you'll think of me – I should be showing you round.'

'What you could do with is a cup of something,' said Sandra, with decision. 'I'll get it for you – what would you like – tea – coffee? Don't worry, I can find the kitchen.'

'I'd love a cup of tea. Everything's just through there – to your right –' Mrs Wilkins raised her head, then dropped back against her chair. 'There's a mug or two still around – near the cooker –'

After watching her for a moment or two, Trevor asked if she hadn't got someone to help her. 'None of my business, I know, but can't your husband give you a hand? Bit hard for you on your own –'

There was a silence. He thought perhaps she hadn't heard him (Sandra was making enough noise in the kitchen for a rodeo), then he thought, Christ, maybe she's a One Parent Family, oh, trust me – but at last she said in a low voice:

'My husband's in hospital, Mr Bennett.'

'Oh. Very sorry to hear that, Mrs Wilkins. Nothing serious, is it?'

'He – broke his leg.'

Nothing too tragic. Trevor was relieved. The way those great dark eyes were looking at him, he'd thought – well, he didn't know what – but a broken leg – that wasn't so bad –

'Playin' soccer, was it?'

'What?'

'Was he playing football – when he broke his leg?'

'No.' Mrs Wilkins sat up as Sandra, flushed with success, bore in two mugs of tea. 'Oh, this is so kind, Mrs Bennett – thank you –'

'Call me Sandra. Mrs Bennett means Trevor's Mum to me and like her I'm not. Trevor, your tea's on the sink unit. Go and have a look at the kitchen – it's gorgeous!'

Mrs Wilkins smiled. 'I'm Eleanor, then. You know, you really are kind – I do appreciate this.'

'No trouble. Did you want sugar? We don't take it, but I couldn't find any anyway.'

'No – no, I don't.' Eleanor sipped her tea and began to look a little less pale, a little less weary. 'You liked the kitchen, then?'

'It's great. Really great. Well, everything is. Just what we wanted.'

'You think you'll take the flat?'

'Too right. We're lucky to get it at what they're askin'. Place like Graymeads ... Soon as we got here and I saw they had *wallflowers* out the front, I said to Trevor, "This is for me," and he agreed.'

Eleanor Wilkins gave a strange little sigh and finished her tea; she said nothing, and Sandra, after a pause, looked uneasily round for Trevor. 'Trev! Trev! What you doin' out there? I told you your tea was on the sink unit!'

He came in, smiling. 'Just lookin' round. Smashin' pad, eh, Sandra? Want to take it?'

She jumped up and went to him. 'I've just been tellin' Eleanor here we're lucky to get it. Do you think we could see the bedrooms now, Eleanor?'

'Oh, of course – I'll show you –'

'Don't get up. We can manage.'

'No, I'd better come – just have to take my time –'

There were two bedrooms, one, as Eleanor had said, full of packing cases, the other, the larger of the two, as neat and impersonal as the sittingroom, with a made-up double bed, a fitted wall cupboard and a couple of chairs. One wall held a wide window with venetian blinds, the others – Sandra gave a cry of surprise –

'Oh, look at the walls, Trev! One white, one pink, one green!'

'Avocado,' said Eleanor, tonelessly.

'Avocado?'

'I believe the shade – was called Avocado.'

'All looks like Neapolitan ice cream to me,' said Trevor, and Sandra frowned and apologised; Eleanor would have to forgive him; he didn't mean to be rude.

'That's all right, we didn't do these walls. They were like that when we came in. The Graymeads agent said people could decorate as they liked.' Eleanor laughed, uneasily. 'I suppose our predecessors couldn't make up their minds.'

'I prefer one colour meself,' said Sandra. 'What do you think, Trev?'

'Doesn't bother me, I don't know one colour from another. But we could change it any time. No problem.'

'No!' Eleanor's tone was sharp. 'I shouldn't do that. I mean – don't do any decorating.'

'Why not? Trev's a dab hand.' Sandra gave him a radiant smile. 'What've you got against decorating?'

Eleanor sank down into a bedroom chair, her face pale again, her breath coming quickly. 'I suppose I'm just being superstitious. It was when he was beginning to do this room that my husband – had his accident.'

'Oh, I'm sorry, I didn't know –'

'He broke his leg,' Trevor told Sandra. 'Eleanor said, when you were makin' the tea. What did he do, then? Fall off the ladder?'

'That's right.' As suddenly as she had turned pale, Eleanor coloured, the flush rising to the roots of her red-blonde hair. 'What made it worse was that we were arguing at the time. Not that that was anything new ... We were arguing about the colours here. I said avocado, he said pink – oh, it was so silly ... Before he could do anything, he fell. And that was horrible.' She put her hand to her eyes and slowly and quietly began to weep. 'Horrible – it was horrible.'

'Don't, love,' cried Sandra, going to her, 'Don't upset yourself. Think of the baby. It's all over now.'

'All over?' Eleanor took her hands from her eyes and stared into their faces with such desolate intensity they looked away. 'Oh, yes, it's all over. Tony's left me. He doesn't want to see me again, ever. Why should he? I pushed him off the ladder. He might have broken his neck.'

*

'We'll still take it, won't we?' asked Sandra, running again to keep up with Trevor, 'I mean, we'd be crazy not to – a lovely flat like that –'

'I don't fancy it.'

'Trev, we might never get another chance!'

'So what? I don't fancy sleepin' in that bloody awful Neapolitan bedroom.'

'You said the colours didn't matter to you, you don't care about them, I know you don't – you're thinkin' about her, aren't you?'

His handsome face was cold and set as he pressed the button for the lift. 'She seemed nice,' he muttered. 'Sort of gentle. And all the time – you can't trust anybody, can you?'

'She's sorry enough now.'

'Too late. The bloke's got some sense – he's scarpered.' Trevor shook his head, as the lift bore them quietly away from the fourth floor. 'But what a temper, eh? Scares the pants off me to think of it, her doin' a thing like that.'

'Why are we talkin' about her?' asked Sandra. 'We're what

counts. It's what we want that matters.'

'And you want us to take that flat?'

'Yes, I do. What they did – what she did – 's got nothing to do with us, Trev. We shouldn't give them another thought.'

'OK, OK, if it's what you want – Only, stop looking at me like that.'

'As long as we trust each other, Trev?'

'We trust each other.' He stopped to kiss her pretty, upturned face and she put her arms around him and held him close. That afternoon he rang the Graymeads agent and said they would take Flat 51. They agreed to move in the following week.

*

Sandra described herself as over the moon. Trevor said nothing. Only looked. Looked – what? Sandra said she just wished he would stop it.

'Stop what?'

'Lookin' the way you do.'

'I can't help the way I look.'

'You know what I mean.'

They faced each other over the cases they were unpacking in the main bedroom and anger suddenly crackled between them like summer lightning. 'I mean, looking depressed,' cried Sandra. 'As though there was something wrong.'

'I'm not. You're imaginin' it.'

'I am *not* imaginin' it! You're just tryin' to spoil my pleasure in this place, aren't you? You've been like a wet weekend ever since we decided to take it and now we're in you're worse. What's up with you?'

'There's nothing up with *me*.'

'You're sayin' it's my fault you're so down in the mouth?'

'I'm not bloody down anywhere.' Trevor flung himself out of the bedroom into the small hallway. 'To hell with it – It's your fault we're here, anyway, you can't deny that. I'm off.'

'Where? Where you goin'? There's nowhere round here.'

'There's a pub.'

Sandra's round young face crumpled. 'You're goin' to the pub? Without me, Trev? You've never done that before.'

'Always a first time.' He gave her a hard cold stare. 'See you.'

'What about the unpackin'? We've only just started, there's all them boxes in the kitchen – And I was just gonna do some supper for you –'

'Oh, yes? You mean open a few tins, same as usual? No thanks, darlin'. I'll go down the pub and get a sandwich. Or mebbe I can find a Chinese – Don't wait up.'

The flat door banged behind him. Sandra was alone.

The journey from moon to earth had never been faster. She sat on an upturned box in the hall and gave herself up to the luxury of a good cry; then she returned to the bedroom and tried to finish unpacking the suitcases. But where was the point? If she and Trev were havin' a row ... ? Why not just leave the unpacking? Leave everything? Nothing mattered. If she and Trevor were rowin' ...

She lay on the bed which she had not yet made up and lit a cigarette. Blew smoke. Looked at the ceiling. Looked at the walls. One pink. One white. One avocado. She gave a shudder, thought – 'There's something wrong with those colours. They don't look like Neapolitan ice cream. Don't look like anything so nice. Give you the creeps, don't they? No wonder Trevor –' She wouldn't think of him, she would not think of him – Tomorrow lunchtime she would go see if she could find some cheap emulsion. The room was crying out to be all one colour. Avocado. Anybody with any colour sense could see that and Trevor needn't think that she would change her mind, because Trevor had no colour sense and never had had and as soon as he came back she would tell him so, she would tell him just what she was planning to do – Tears filled her eyes again and she drew for comfort on her cigarette. *If* he came back –

He came. Full of contrition. Gathered her in his arms and swore never to upset her again. It had all been his fault. It would never happen again.

'I promise, I promise,' he murmured, kissing her, holding her. 'Never again, Sandra, never again.'

'And you didn't mean that about my cookin', did you? I mean, we've just moved in, I've got to open tins, I'm not straightened out, I haven't got me freezer workin', or anything. I don't usually open tins, do I?'

'Course you don't. You're a smashin' cook. I don't know why I said that, I don't, honest.'

'So you won't mind if I open one now?'

'I'll open it for you. I'll get you supper tonight. Beans and eggs and bacon – because I'm starvin' anyway.'

'You didn't get a Chinese?'

'No.' He gave a slow grin. 'It'd have choked me. Look, you're worn out, love. Why don't you turn in and I'll bring you a tray to bed, if I can find a tray.'

'No,' said Sandra, at once. She looked uneasily round the bedroom, at the strange walls, moving, pressing – 'No, it'll be easier in the kitchen, Trevor.'

'It's full of packing cases.'

'I know, but it'll be better. We can cook the meal together.' Trevor bent to kiss her again. 'Anything you say, Sandra, anything you say.'

Over the meal she told him of her plan for making the bedroom all one colour.

'All avocado?' Trevor raised his eyebrows. 'Since when have you been keen on green?'

'I've always liked green.'

'Leave it off. You told me once you wanted a pink bedroom. Pink and feminine, you said, and I said no way if it had to be mine as well and where was all your women's lib? Don't you remember that?'

'I may have said that some time but now I've seen that bedroom I think it should be all avocado. Don't you agree?'

'I don't care what colour you choose,' he replied, stretching out for her hand and gazing fondly into her eyes. 'As long as you have what you want, Sandra, that's fine with me.'

'Oh, Trevor ... I never thought I'd hear you talk to me like that again!'

'I mean it. What you want, I want. It's as simple as that.'

But in the night Trevor woke Sandra and told her that he couldn't sleep. 'It's this room,' he muttered. 'Seems sort of heavy – weighs you down – I've been thinkin', mebbe it should be pink, after all. I don't really go for that avocado. Tomorrow lunchtime I'll see if I can pick up some cans of emulsion and we'll make it all one colour. Pink. Goodnight, Sandra.'

'Goodnight,' she whispered, and lay staring into the darkness.

In the event, neither of them bought any paint.

'Weren't you goin' to get some avocado emulsion?' asked Trevor, as they finished a strenuous evening's work of unpacking and sorting out.

'Weren't you goin' to buy pink?' countered Sandra.

'When did I say I wanted pink paint?'

'In the night. Don't you remember? You woke me up and said you wanted to do the bedroom pink.'

'Never! You must have been dreamin'. I thought we'd agreed to do it your way.'

'I'll make coffee,' said Sandra. As she filled the kettle, her hands were trembling.

'You OK?' asked Trevor, watching her.

'Bit tired. It's all this unpacking' ... bein' upside down ... I never could stand not bein' straight. Wish now I'd let Mum come over to give us a hand.'

'We're best on our own. She'd have found fault with everything we've done.'

'She wouldn't, she's not like that. Anyway, I didn't ask her, did I? Oh, but it'll be lovely when we're straight, won't it, Trevor? Really straight?'

'Stop worryin' about it. See what's on the telly. I've had enough.'

They both felt strangely apprehensive.

*

And they never did get straight. Not 'really', as Sandra put it. Perhaps because they could not bring themselves to do anything about the walls in their bedroom, those sinister pink, green and white ice cream walls. What a load of rubbish ... As though those walls could have anything to do with anything ... But Eleanor Wilkins' face danced more and more often before Sandra's eyes these days, a white, white, face, with dark, dark eyes ... 'We were arguing about the colours here ... I said avocado, he said pink ...' Then, 'Horrible ... it was horrible ...' Horrible, horrible, horrible ...

'Why don't we paint the whole thing white?' cried Sandra

to herself. 'Plain white?' But she could never put the suggestion into words, could never say, white – avocado – pink – There was no way out, no way out at all.

Then Trevor started drinking.

*

'If it's as bad as you say, love, you should come home,' Sandra's mother said indignantly on one of her frequent telephone calls. 'Has he started knockin' you about yet?'

'No, of course not. Trev's not like that. He just – well, I dunno – I can't do anything right, that's all. He can't seem to stop – gettin' at me.'

'We never liked him, you know, your Dad and me. Never had a bit of time for him.'

'You never said. You never said you didn't like Trevor.'

'Didn't want to hurt you, did we? He was your choice. But we knew you'd find him out one day, oh, yes.'

'We've always been so happy, Mum, we really have. Until now.'

'Yes, well what you ought to do is get to know some more people and go out yourself. There must be plenty of nice young folk in them flats you're in now.'

'In Graysmead? You must be joking. There's none of 'em young and they're all toffee nosed. If they see you in the lift they don't speak to you. They never call, never want to know. I reckon you could die here and they'd never notice.'

'What a thing to say, Sandra! Look, shall I come over? Tomorrow afternoon? I could easily leave your Dad's tea, get the half past one bus and be with you by two?'

'I'm out at work, remember?'

'Well, in the evenin', then. I could come tonight.'

'No, it's all right, Mum, thanks. I might go to a film. One of the girls at the shop asked me if I'd go with her.'

'Oh, well, that's good. Let him see you're not bothered, you've other things to do, that's the secret. Let him see you don't care and he'll come runnin'. Men are often a bit difficult when they first get married, you know – don't like bein' tied.'

'Mum, we lived together for two years before we got married.'

'That's not the same thing at all. A man can walk out any time –'

'And so can I, walk out.' Sandra sniffed. 'Only, of course, I never would. Oh, I don't think our troubles 've got anything to do with our marriage, Mum. It's to do with the bedroom. It's the wrong colours.'

'It's what?'

'Nothing. I'll be in touch.'

'And have a nice evenin' at the pictures, love. Don't forget what I told you – let him see –'

'Goodnight, Mum. Thanks.'

*

There was of course no film, no girl from the shop to go out with; she'd just said that to keep her mother happy and to stop her from coming round and giving advice for the rest of the evening. There would be a soap on the telly she didn't want to see, there would be too many cigarettes, there would be the long long wait for Trevor to come home, the anxiety to see how he would be –

'Where've we gone wrong, Trev?' Sandra murmured, dully. 'Is it us? Or, that room?' She lit a cigarette, tried to laugh. 'Or, am I paranoid?' It wasn't funny.

Then the telephone rang.

'Sandra? Do you remember me?' It was Eleanor Wilkins.

Remember her? Sandra stubbed out her cigarette with trembling fingers and grasped the handset to her as though it were some sort of lifebelt.

'How are you?' she asked, hoarsely. 'Did you – have the baby?'

'Oh, yes.' Eleanor laughed. 'She's beautiful, Sandra, really beautiful. We've called her Melissa.'

'That's great. I'm happy for you.' Sandra hesitated. 'You said – we?'

'Yes, I wanted to tell you.' Eleanor's voice was soft and contented, rich, thick cream, pouring. 'Tony and me – we're back together. He came to see me when I'd had the baby – in plaster still – hobbling – oh, I felt so terrible – But as soon as we saw each other again, it was just – as though we'd never been apart. That time in between, Sandra – it never happened.'

'That time in between – was when you were here, wasn't it? In the flat?'

'Yes. The bad time.'

'Horrible,' whispered Sandra. 'Horrible ...'

'Oh, no,' said Eleanor. 'Not you too?'

When Sandra had talked, talked herself dry, Eleanor said there was only one thing they could do. Leave. As soon as possible.

'How can we?'

'Give notice, pack up, go. Where's the problem?'

'But go where?'

'Anywhere, it doesn't matter. I'm not joking, Sandra, it's the only thing to save your marriage.'

'You really think – it's the bedroom?'

'I know it sounds crazy – Oh, just tell Trevor what I've said and get out while you can. Where is he now?'

'Where he usually is. Down the pub. Situation normal.'

'He didn't go drinking before?'

'Hardly at all. Didn't care about it.'

'You see?' cried Eleanor, her voice now high and trembling. 'It's just what happened to Tony and me ... Please, Sandra, don't talk any more. Go and find Trevor and leave. Now, Keep in touch, though, won't you? Sandra, keep in touch?'

But Sandra was already on her way.

*

There was only one pub near Graymeads – The Grenadier. Sandra had been in once or twice when Trevor had taken her in the early days and knew Dora, the barmaid slightly; she felt she might just dare to slide into the Lounge Bar and ask her if she'd seen Trevor without drawing too much attention to herself – ribald remarks from the fellows he'd got to know, she could do without.

'Looking for Trev, dear?' It was too easy. Dora's quick grey eyes had spotted her as soon as she had come through the doors. 'He's just gone, dear.'

'Gone?'

'He was a bit merry, dear. Thought he ought to get on home – he'd things to do. I expect he's already there, waiting for you.'

Sandra flew back to Graymeads on wings. Trevor was at home, waiting for her, she would be able to tell him what Eleanor had told her, he would be able to see that their marriage could be put right the minute they packed their bags and walked out of Number 51. Oh, thank God, thank God, it was not going to be too late.

But in the hall of the flat she was brought up short by the sight of several large cans of emulsion paint. She looked at the labels. The paint was pink.

*

'That you, Sandra?'

Trevor appeared in the doorway of the bedroom; he was carrying a roller already wet with paint and was – not merry – quite drunk.

'Where've you been, Sandra?'

'To look for you. We had a telephone call.'

'Call?' He looked at her, suspiciously. 'Who from?'

'Mrs Wilkins.'

The reply was so unexpected it seemed to sober him a little, as though the name had penetrated the mists of alcohol that separated him from her and allowed him to see Sandra for a moment clearly.

'Mrs Wilkins? Eleanor?'

'That's right. Listen, Trev, I've got to talk to you. It's very very important –'

But the mists were closing around him again. He shook his head.

'Gotta get on, Sandra. Got this paint, you see. From the DIY ... Late night shoppin' ... cheap ... Gotta do that bedroom.'

'No, Trev.' She ran to him, grasped his arm which wavered and sent pink paint slopping down her jacket. 'No, listen, you're not goin' to paint that bedroom. You're not goin' to touch it. I know what that place can do to people. It changes them. Makes them wild, violent – It made Eleanor and Tony like that, it'll make us the same – Trevor!'

He was ignoring her, pushing her away from him, staring ahead with eyes glazed, malevolent. 'That room's goin' to be pink!' he shouted, 'So get away from me, Sandra! Get the hell out of my way.'

'No!' She ran after him into the bedroom, forgetting suddenly all that she wanted to tell him. 'If it's goin' to be anything, it'll be avocado.' Yes, that was all that mattered. 'Avocado, Trevor! Not pink – avocado!'

'We'll see about that.'

They faced each other across the bed which Sandra noted had been covered by Trevor with one of their best wedding present sheets; both were breathing quickly with little shallow gasps that seemed to bring no air, and now Sandra could smell the staleness of the beer on Trevor's breath, his sweat as he waved the roller close to her face. She tore off her jacket and pushed up the sleeves of her blouse.

'Give me that roller, Trevor. Give it here!'

'Like hell, I will.'

'I'm not goin' to let you do it, Trevor. I've said all along that this room should be avocado and that's what it's goin' to be. So, give me the roller.'

He laughed. 'Stupid cow. What makes you think I'd do anything you wanted? See them steps I've put there? See that paint? Think I'm goin' to waste all the cash I've spent to let you do what you want? You always were as thick as two planks, but if you think you can stop me, you're dafter than I thought. Get out the way!' He came round the bed towards her, still waving the roller at her. 'Get out the way, I said. I'm goin' to do that wall.'

'You're not, Trev. You are not paintin' this wall. You are not paintin' this wall PINK.'

'I'm not?' He laughed again and held the roller to her brow so that it dripped paint down her cheek; his eyes were dark, hard, and menacing, a stranger's eyes. 'Who's goin' to stop me? You?' She made a grab at the roller as it passed before her eyes, but missed, then Trevor threw it down and hit her brutally on the side of the face with his fist. She screamed; paint was in her eyes now, in her mouth, and blood too. 'Trevor –' She tried to say his name but he hit her again, this time knocking her to the floor where she lay without moving.

'You?' repeated Trevor. 'You are goin' to stop me? That's a laugh, isn't it?'

He turned aside, staggering, and put his hands to his head which had begun to throb. 'Gotta finish this room ... gotta make it pink ... Blast Sandra ... silly little bitch.' He looked back at her still figure and an unpleasant thought pushed its way into his mind. Had he hit her too hard? No, she was OK. Putting it on. Trying to make him feel sorry. As though he would. She had it coming, deserved all she got, goin' on and on ... 'This room's got to be avocado ... I'm not goin' to let you do it, Trevor ...' Avocado ... He spat. 'We'll see whether it's goin' to be avocado, or not.'

He made a run at the opened can of paint he had left near the door, thrust the roller into it and staggered back to the stepladder. 'See what colour this is, Sandra? Pink. Pink, pink, pink ...' Breathing heavily, he yanked the legs of the ladder apart so that their cords were taut and then began to climb unsteadily up the steps. 'Do the top. Better do the top. Shoulda done it first ... Oh, hell, so what? What's the difference? All pink, anyway. Pink, bloody pink. Hear that, Sandra? Pink, pink, pink!'

Sandra's eyelids slowly lifted but she saw nothing; she was only conscious of pain, searing pain in her head and of the salt taste of blood in her mouth. A voice a long way off was droning, 'Hear that, Sandra? Pink, bloody pink. Pink, pink, pink ...'

Pink?

Her eyes were beginning to focus as true consciousness returned and she struggled into a sitting position. Trevor was on a step ladder, swinging crazily as he dabbed a dripping roller in the direction of a green wall, and he was crooning to himself, over and over, 'Pink, pink, pink, this wall's goin' to be pink, it's all goin' to be pink ... Hear that, Sandra? Pink. All pink.'

Hatred filled Sandra, hatred for that silly, idiotic figure on the steps. She knew now that she had hated him for years. All the long craven years of their marriage when he had knocked out of her any love she might ever have had for him. They'd always been wrong for each other, from the very beginning. She'd known within a week that the whole thing had been one sickening mistake, yet when she'd asked for a divorce, he'd said, no, they could still make a go of it, and she'd listened and gone on hoping ... No, that wasn't true. She hadn't hoped. What was there left for her to hope for? A smile twisted her bruised lip. She'd been afraid, that was all. It had been easier just to carry on, living with things the way they were, rather than risking she didn't know what. But tonight was different. Tonight she was prepared to risk anything. Because tonight she'd had enough. Tonight he had hit her for the last time.

She couldn't walk to the ladder but she could crawl there and when she reached it, with all the strength she could find, she jerked at the cords keeping the supports apart. As she felt the ladder shake above her, as she felt its collapse and his harsh cry as he felt himself going, going, she pulled herself away and laughed. Laughed as his body hit the floor and his voice was stilled. Then she too lay still.

*

'It wasn't my fault,' said Mrs Manning, the fretful tenant of Number 50. 'Though I know I should have said something. I admit that. But I didn't like to. I mean, it wasn't up to me, was it?'

'You knew there'd been accidents here,' said the police inspector, mildly. 'A word wouldn't have done any harm.'

'But I didn't know Mr and Mrs Bennett, Inspector! None of us did. I mean, we like to keep ourselves to ourselves, at Graymeads, that's always been the way. If you're speaking to the other folk round here, I'm sure you'll get told the same.'

'I'm sure I shall, Mrs Manning. Still, didn't that second accident strike you as a bit of a coincidence?'

'Well, that's what we thought it was. Coincidence. What else could it have been? The Clarkes were both dead. They couldn't have had anything to do with what happened to the Wilkins pair.'

'Any more than the Wilkins couple could have had anything to do with what happened to the Bennetts? Tell me about the Clarkes, Mrs Manning.'

Mrs Manning looked uneasily around her immaculate sittingroom. 'Awful people,' she whipered. 'Awful, Inspector. Well, he was. A really brutal ugly sort of man. Not the sort who should ever have come here in the first place. So we others thought.'

'What was his job?'

'Painter and decorator.'

The inspector and the constable exchanged glances. 'Some decorator,' said the constable, grinning.

'Yes, that was the funny thing,' said Mrs Manning. 'I believe he was reckoned to be quite good at his job. He only did that room like that to spite her. She told him she hated it, they had a terrible row.'

'She told you, did she?'

'Oh, no, I didn't know her. Not to talk to. One of my friends went collecting one day and Mrs Clarke asked her in, to wait while she found change, you know, and she showed my friend the bedroom then. She said, didn't she think it was terrible, would anyone in their senses want those three walls like that, and she was going to make him do it all over again. Avocado.'

'And when he was doing this repainting, he fell off the ladder?'

'Pushed, wasn't he? Mrs Clarke pushed him, didn't she?' Mrs Manning licked her lips. 'Because he was doing it pink.'

'That was never established, Mrs Manning. The inquest verdict was accidental death.'

'Well, I didn't see her do it –' Mrs Manning's pale eyes darted between the expressionless faces of the two policemen. 'But if you'd heard the ROW that was going on – "It'll be pink! No, avocado! I say, *pink*! I say, *avocado*!" Oh, they were really screaming at each other, just like they always did, because she could give as good as she got until he hit her. I could always tell when he'd hit her because then she'd be quiet.' Mrs Manning shuddered. 'Poor thing, you couldn't help feeling sorry for her. Plain little creature, she was, too ... Hair always looked as if it needed washing.'

'You often heard them quarrelling, then?'

'Like I said, all the time. I used to wish I could say something, but of course I couldn't.'

'You didn't give evidence at the inquest, did you, Mrs Manning? Didn't say you'd heard them quarrelling on the night of the accident?'

'No one asked me to.' She lowered her eyes. 'Anyway, I wasn't here. I had to go to my sister's in Leeds. I didn't come back until after the inquest.'

'And then you were told that Mrs Clarke had died too, in hospital?'

'Yes, Pneumonia. Because she'd lain so long.'

'Before she was found.' Inspector Arnott's gaze rested sombrely on Mrs Manning's puckered features. 'Not pleasant, is it, to think of her lying there all night beside a man with a fractured skull? Ever think you might have called earlier, Mrs Manning?'

'I called the next time,' she said, hurriedly. 'It was me found Mr and Mrs Wilkins, you know. I got the ambulance for them. *And* for the Bennetts. You might say, I *saved* the Bennetts, Inspector!'

'But if you'd told the Bennetts –'

'Told them what? Told them what, Inspector?'

'God knows,' he replied and closed his notebook with a snap. 'I wish I knew. But somebody should have told them something.'

*

A young couple was standing outside Number 51 as the policemen came out of Mrs Manning's flat. A dark-haired man, a blonde girl.

'Not trying to get in there, are you?' asked Inspector Arnott, 'There's no one in.'

'We're waiting for the agent to show us round. The rent's amazing –'

'I'll bet. The last people who paid that amazing rent are in hospital. Mr Bennett has two fractured ribs, a broken ankle and a broken wrist; Mrs Bennett has cuts and bruises and is suffering from shock. And they're both damned lucky at that. This flat is not available, Mr –'

'Paget. Derek Paget. This is my girlfriend, Emma James. What do you mean, it's not available? We were told –'

'Take my advice,' said the Inspector, kindly. 'Scarper. This flat might have to be closed for some time.'

'But why?' cried the girl. 'You might at least tell us why!'

'I could say – exorcism.' He grinned as he walked away, the constable at his side. 'But we'll call it – redecoration.'

III

Moving Day

R. Chetwynd-Hayes

I went to live with my aunts just before my thirty-fifth birthday.

In fact they were my great-aunts, being the three sisters of my maternal grandmother. The eldest Edith was ninety-eight, the middle one Matilda eighty-seven, the youngest Edna eight-five. My grandmother had rather let the side down by dying at the ridiculously youthful age of eighty-one. Perhaps the fact she was the only one to marry had something to do with that. As I was the only living relative and in consequence the sole heir to whatever estate they eventually left, moving in with them was not such a bad idea. At least so I thought at the time. I would be able to keep an eye on what would one day be my property and make certain that no kindly person tried to ease his or her way into their wills. It has been known to happen.

I had not been in that large, musty, over-furnished and damp-haunted house a week, before I realised the three sisters were – at the very best – looked upon as eccentrics in the neighbourhood and even feared.

Certainly from the very first I had to admit there was an oddness about them that was hard to define. Something to do with the way they walked. A kind of quick-glance-over-the-shoulder-shuffle. Then their pre-occupation with the local churchyard was out of the ordinary.

The only people they seemed to know were there. In the churchyard.

The table talk I endured on my first night put me of the really excellent food. Edna was cook and a very good one she was too.

Moving Day 41

Edith waved a fork at me and said: 'When you move, David, you want to make certain all is ready. The furniture ordered, the box chosen, the wordage composed.'

I smiled gently, assuming old age had muddled her poor old brain. 'But, Auntie, dear, I have just moved. Moved from my bachelor flat into your nice house.'

A genteel titter ran round the table and Edna poked me playfully in the ribs with a dessert spoon. 'You silly boy! We mean when you move into your permanent home. The cosy little nest in the churchyard.'

I made an interesting noise, then tried to adjust my outlook to the exceptionally unusual. 'I see. Be prepared for anything? Eh?'

'He's quite sensible,' Edna informed Edith. 'So many young people these days are apt to treat *moving* with unseemly levity.'

'Takes after his granddad,' Matilda maintained. 'In fact Alfred – did you know, David, that was your grandfather's name? – moved twenty-five years ago last Christmas. He said, "Make certain the lad – you – knows what's what." And I said, "You never need fear about that, Alfred".'

'Only the other day,' Edith stressed, tapping a knife handle on the table, 'you forgot to mention Alfred said that only the other day.'

'I hadn't forgotten,' Matilda protested, 'I just hadn't got round to it. At the same time as I was going to mention the lovely surprise we've planned for David's birthday.'

Edith shook her head reproachfully. 'Now, you've spoilt it all, Matilda. The fact he now knows a lovely surprise is planned for his birthday, means it will only be half a lovely surprise. He may even guess what it is. If you have a failing, Matilda, it is talking out of turn. Gladys Foot, who you may remember *moved* in 1932, said the same thing only yesterday. "Matilda will talk out of turn," she said. "She even told me when I was going to *move*, and I didn't want to know until a day after the event." '

Matilda dabbed her eyes with a black-edged handkerchief. 'I mean well, Edith. I'm sure dear David won't give the matter of a lovely surprise on his birthday another thought, until he learns what it is on the great day, which I believe is the day after tomorrow.'

Edith hastened to console. 'Don't take on so, dear. I mean I only correct you for your own good. Have a glass of Mortuary 51. It will cheer you up.'

I may as well point out that Mortuary 51 was a rather bad sherry and had nothing to do with a mortuary, but they had churchyard-funeral titles for almost everything. I mean the pepperbox was an earth-sprinkler, potatoes – corpoties, spoons – grave-diggers and any kind of soup or gravy, churchyard bouillon.

When I was escorted to my bedroom by Edna, she assured me that: 'The bed shrouds were changed this morning.'

I lay awake for most of the night trying to understand how this death-related mania had come into being. Possibly their longevity and the fact everyone they had known had died, might have had something to do with it. In the very beginning I mean.

My thirty-fifth birthday will never be forgotten.

To begin I found three black-edged cards propped up against a toast rack on the breakfast table. The goodwill messages were I am certain unique in birthday greeting history.

> Three times thirty-five is one hundred and five,
>   Then you should no longer be alive.
> With luck this could be the last birthday.
>   And that's all we have to say.

> From your loving aunties Edith, Edna and Matilda and all those who have *moved*.

But no present. No lovely surprise.

I had to assume it was the birthday tea that was planned for five o'clock. But I was wrong.

After lunch I was ordered to put on my best suit, polish my shoes and comb my hair, because we were going visiting. The aunts put on black satin dresses, black straw hats, and black button-up boots. Then we all set out, walked the entire length of the High Street, watched I swear by the entire population of the village. Then we turned into a narrow lane, picked our way over puddles, pushed open – or rather Edna did – a low gate and entered the churchyard.

Edith called out, 'Hullo, everybody. Don't worry about us. Won't be long,' then led us along weed-infested paths until we came to that part of the churchyard where those who had reaped a reasonably rich harvest during their day in the earthly vineyard slept the long sleep. Or so I assumed. Marble angels stood guard over miniature flower gardens. Granite headstones proclaimed the virtues of those who rested under marble chips. We stopped at a strip of closely clipped grass, into which at regular intervals had been inserted round lead plaques, all bearing black numbers: 14, 15, 16, 17.

Edna took an envelope from her handbag. 'You see, dear, we have purchased our permanent homes. Here are three deeds which state that plot 14 belongs to Edith, plot 15 belongs to Matilda and plot 16 belongs to me. Eventually we will move into our plots, but you may be sure leave them now and again to see how you are getting on.'

There was really no answer for that one, so I kept quiet and displayed more interest in the empty plots than I actually felt. Then Edna produced the fourth deed.

'Now, dear, we come to your lovely birthday surprise. We have all clubbed together and brought you plot 17. You too now own your permanent home. What have you to say about that?'

All three looked at me with such an air of joyful expectancy, I just had to express delight – near ecstasy – happy surprise, even if it did mean gabbling insane nonsense.

'How can I thank you – something I've always wanted – I will treasure it for as long as I live – and longer. I can't wait to get into it ...'

'We had thought,' Matilda said, 'of tying a greetings present card to the plot number, but Edith thought it wouldn't be respectful. Now, Edna, make the presentation in the proper way.'

Edna straightened up and stood rather like a soldier at attention, the little slip of paper in her hand. It was in fact a receipt for five pounds. She raised her voice until it was in danger of dissolving into a rasping croak.

'I hereby bestow on my beloved great-nephew David Greenfield the deeds of his permanent home, trusting he will lie in it with credit to his noble *moved-on* ones.'

I accepted the 'deeds' and said thank you very much several times, having exhausted my fund of grateful words in the acceptance speech.

Then we all sang the first verse of 'Abide with Me' before starting the tramp back to the village, bestowing words of farewell on to most of the graves as we went. I became acutely aware of the considerable crowd that had collected just beyond the churchyard wall, some of which gave gratuitous advice that included, 'Why don't yer stay there?', 'Dig hard and hearty and bed down', 'Set up house there', 'Yer all dead, why don't yer lie down?'

However all this came to an abrupt end when Matilda pointed two rigid fingers at the crowd and chanted in a shrill voice:

> On ye all the evil eye.
> By Beldaza ye all die.
> If ye not gone in one mo.
> Or before I wriggle big toe.

And they all went. Running, jumping, pushing, gasping; I have never before or since seen a crowd that included quite a number of elderly people move so fast, or with such agility.

Edna sighed deeply. 'What a shame, sisters, we have to frighten people so much. I'd much rather be friendly and explain all about *moving* over a cup of tea and a condensed milk sandwich.'

'The price of being special,' Edith explained.

'The curse of being upper,' Matilda agreed.

'I do hope we don't have to become too drastic,' Edna had the last word. 'People should only *move* when it's right and proper.'

*

Two weeks later Edith was taken ill.

Not exactly ill, rather taken faint. She wilted and took to her bed and I slowly became aware that the house was being invaded.

Sort of.

Matilda and Edna accentuated their quick-glance-over-one-shoulder shuffle, only the quick glance was not so quick anymore. There was an awful lot of whispering too. I couldn't catch all of it, but what I did seemed very ordinary. 'How are you, dear? Doesn't seem a year since you *moved*. Yes time does fly. Shouldn't be long now before your Tom starts turning up his toes ...'

Another thing. I began to take quick glances over my shoulder, for there was the distinct impression that someone was standing way back and a quick turning of the head enabled me to catch the merest glimpse of him. Not sufficient to register any details, but enough to send a cold shiver down my spine.

As time passed – three days or more – impressions began to set into near certainties. I distinctly saw the back of a woman attired in a polka dot muslin dress disappear round the corner of the landing, which led to Edith's bedroom. When I turned the same corner some ten seconds later there was no one in sight. I peeped into Aunt Edith's bedroom, she was lying still with hands crossed, but otherwise the room was empty.

Twice I was awakened in the middle of the night by cold lips kissing my forehead. Once by cold fingers gently caressing my throat. When I complained to Matilda and Edna next morning, both giggled and Matilda said, 'Martha Longbridge always had an affectionate nature,' and Edna added, 'Daphne is so mischievous.'

I asked, 'Who are Martha and Daphne?' and they both gave me a pitying smile, before Edna replied:

'Two old friends who *moved* a long time ago.'

I did not dare ask any more questions.

Three weeks after Edith had been taken faint, she died. At least I would have said she died, the two remaining sisters insisted she had merely prepared herself for *moving*. Not *moved* you understand. Stopped breathing so as to *prepare* for *moving*.

The funeral took place three days later and was a very sparse affair. The coffin was pushed to the churchyard on a hand bier – rather like a costermonger's barrow – and the clergyman was not encouraged to linger once he had galloped his way through the burial service. A deep grave had been dug in plot 14 and Edith's cheap pine coffin was lowered into it, then the earth shovelled back in and piled up as an untidy hump, which Edna crowned by a jam jar containing three marigolds. One from each of us. Then we went home to roast beef, Yorkshire pudding, roast potatoes (corpoties), Brussels sprouts and rich churchyard bouillon, followed by apple pie and custard.

The house ceased to be invaded. The unseen guests merely settled in.

By that I mean I only occasionally felt the urge to glance quickly over the left shoulder, but really had the heebies when I woke up and found something very cold in bed with me. According to Edna, this was Susan Cornwall who had been – and presumably still was – very lustful. Needless to say she had *moved* a long time ago.

But the two sisters became very preoccupied and rarely seemed to have time to spare for me. The word *moving* became commonplace.

'We'll talk about that, dear, after the *moving*.'

'Come and see me after the *moving*, dear.'

And when I asked what *moving* entailed, I was told:

'You'll know afterwards, dear.'

May I belatedly explain that all three sisters had always looked elderly, but more due to dress and deportment than physical appearance. Edith of course had looked the older because she was and ninety-eight is a burden of years to carry about. The other two were fairly tall and gaunt, but could easily be taken for ladies in their middle to late sixties.

That was before Edith died.

The interval that separated Edith's death and her *moving* seemed to age them dreadfully. From lean they became emaciated. Eyes sank, teeth were bared in the likeness of a maniac's grin, bones became merely a framework to support brown wrinkled skin. This deterioration was explained by Edna in the following words:

'We both give a bit, dear, so as to make a whole. One day you will have to give for both of us.'

The atmosphere both in the house and in the village was pretty grim, and after the episode of my waking to find something very cold in bed with me, I did begin to entertain ideas about moving out, but – greed is a great courage maker. I found I was one hundred and twenty-five thousand pounds the richer by Edith's death and I stood to gain twice as much when the other two sisters *moved*, so I prayed for the preservation of my sanity and stood firm if not steady.

I suppose it must have been two weeks after the funeral when I began to realise that the vicar was hanging around the street in which the house stood, and could sometimes be seen taking a long time to tie up a shoelace on the other side of the road, ready to bolt should either of the great-aunts appear, but succumb to an attack of nods, winks and head jerking whenever I put foot over the front doorstep.

His name was Humphrey Mondale, tall, thin and bald; a twisted stick of a man, who jerked in a forwardly direction rather than walked, and looked even more eccentric than the two remaining sisters. It was he who had galloped through the burial service on the occasion of Edith's funeral. I kept well clear of him.

But one morning he sprang out on me from the passage that ran between the post office and the public library and had a numbing grip on my left arm before I could get away.

I think he either suffered from chronic catarrh or a perpetual bad head cold, for he spoke with a thick voice and sometimes blurred his syllables.

'Must twalk,' he insisted, his head jerking from side to side on his thin neck, so I was reminded of a ventriloquist's dummy when the head is pushed up to high. 'Nephoo ... yes?'

I said I was the nephew of the two maiden ladies who lived in Moss House, but he did not allow me to finish.

'Twying to contact your for deys. Must stop *moving*. Turrible effect on local people. No one come to church for years. Churchyard shunned. Bishop won't lesson.'

I am one of those people who have a low sales' resistance and once button-holed find it very difficult to get away. The fellow insisted I go with him to the vicarage and what is more hung on to me like grim death to make certain I did. There a female counterpart of himself – plus an untidy mop of grey hair – was introduced as his sister. She gave me a strange look, crossed her two thumbs and said: 'Not me as a good Christian woman, you don't,' then ran into a small kitchen, from which she presently emerged carrying two mugs of weak tea.

Mr Mondale pulled me into a room he called his den – tired

old armchairs, a battered desk, plus for some reason the smell of stale urine and green water.

I sank into a chair which instantly groaned and tried to do something dreadful to me with a broken spring. We didn't say a great deal until his sister had served the weak tea, but I then managed to muster some indignant resolution and asked:

'What is all this about, Mr Mondale? You dragged me in off the street, without so much as by your leave.'

The tea must have done something for his cold for his speech delivery improved.

'Distant member of the family myself, you know. Otherwise I'd have been moved long ago. You know the village is terrified of your aunts. Fear takes many forms. That scene by the churchyard the other day was one. But one day the aunts will really let rip – and then I'd hate to thunk what would happen. Particularly after a *moving*.'

Curiosity got the better of irritation and I leaned forward to ask the all important question:

'What the hell – beg pardon – is this *moving*? They won't tell me a thing. I thought they meant the actual moment of death, or even possibly the funeral. But apparently there's something more.'

The vicar leaned back in his chair and yawned at the ceiling in an effort to emphasise there was indeed more. Much more.

'Good ... good Guard, yes. My word yes. It's the *moving* which upsets the village and will in time bring the newspaper people – especially that Sunday lot – beating a trail to our doors. Fortunately it takes place at night and most people close their curtains and try to ignore what's going on. Two years ago a foolhardy youth did come out and *saw*. He hasn't spoken since and has dreadful fits of the shakes to this day.'

I dragged my chair forward. 'But ... but ... what did he *see*?'

The Reverend Mr Mondale put out a hand. It was not particularly clean and the nails needed trimming.

'Does that member shake?'

'No.'

'Would you say that is a steady hand with not a tremor about it?'

'I would indeed.'

'Surely that is evidence enough that I have never been such

a fool as to peer through parted curtains when your aunts and *that which is with them* pass the house.'

'Then you don't know?'

He jerked his head forward twice, his bad cold losing out to the strong emotion that now held his entire body in a masterly grip.

'I can surmise, sir. I am not the only one who has had the merest glimpse of those who sometimes stray back from the grave and pay a social call on your aunts. Unfortunately churchyards have become associated with certain supernatural nastiness in the public mind. Can it be wondered at, that if at times, in some particular locality, the seeds of that nastiness come to full fruition? Eh?'

I felt a need to confess, share a fear that up to that moment I had not been aware existed.

'There's a nasty atmosphere in the house. Things lurking behind the left shoulder – something cold in the bed – cold fingers on the throat, whispers in the dark.'

The vicar raised both hands, then let them fall back on to the desk with a kind of soggy thump. 'Ah! Then it was not imagination! I have seen white faces with runny eyes looking down from the upper windows! There is only one answer. That house must be razed to the ground and the ground itself sewn with salt.'

'Look here, I'm going to inherit that house!'

'Could you live there after the remaining aunts have *moved*?'

'No, I'd sell it. Good development land.'

Now the vicar raised his eyes ceilingward. 'There is no piercing the armour of the mercenary ungodly.'

I rose. 'Thank you for all you have *not* told me.'

*

I became more unhappy as the days passed, even more so when told Aunt Edith's *moving* day would be the coming Thursday.

Thursday has always been my unlucky day, I will probably die on a Thursday – and be *moved* the following Thursday.

Edna laid a loving hand on my shoulder. 'We say day, dear, in fact it's night. Between eleven and twelve in the evening. The best time. The pub has turned out and all honest people are tucked up in bed. Others!' She shook her head, then tucked her chin in. 'Others must take the consequences if they see that which they shouldn't. After all, *moving* is strictly a family affair.'

For the last three days I went for long walks and turned into an opposite direction whenever I saw the Reverend Mondale, for he had now taken to pushing notes through the letter box begging me to burn the house down before the dreaded event, stating that if I didn't, he would, an item of information I felt duty bound to pass on to the aunts.

Edna tut-tutted and Matilda sighed deeply. 'He was always a trial even as a boy. Edna, we can't have Edith upset and besides this house is home for the entire family. There's no help for it ...'

Edna nodded slowly. 'A visit from Cousin Judith.'

'You think that will be sufficient?' Matilda asked with some anxiety.

'Of course. You may remember the year the churchyard was flooded with the overflow from the chemical works?'

'I most certainly do. A disgrace.'

'Well, Cousin Judith has never been quite the same since. She is really in no fit state to visit anyone. Especially a nervous clergyman.'

I had no more trouble from the Reverend Humphrey Mondale. He was found wandering the downs counting his fingers and expressing great surprise that they were all there. His sister was seen dancing naked on the village green singing a tuneless dirge that accompanied words that ran something like this.

> She ain't got no fingers or toes,
> Her ears have gone, so has her nose,
> One leg's turned green, the other blue,
> And both feet are nailed to a horse's shoe.

I actually prayed I would never see Cousin Judith.

The great day dawned clear and bright. Far across the downs a dog barked — always far away — and nearer to hand a cock crowed and set in motion a series of other sounds that included my two great-aunts calling out, 'Happy moving day, Edith,' which was acknowledged by the door of Edith's room slamming all by itself. Well, it must have done. There was no one near it at the time and not so much as a breath of wind.

When I looked out of the window I saw a small army of cats running down the centre of the road, making for the downs. I was afterwards informed they all collected on top of a mound called locally the Giant's Grave, where they howled and spat for most of the day and part of the following night. You can't ignore the fact that cats have a lot of know-how.

The aunts were very busy all day. They took three baths – I only one. Edna baked lots of little round loaves, which she laid out all over the house. And believe me – they all disappeared. Then I was given the job of collecting large bunches of dandelions; they were mashed into a pulp in the kitchen sink, then boiled in the jam-making saucepan, before being ladled into saucers, which were also laid out all over the house.

And you really must believe me again – every single one was licked clean as Oliver Twist's gruel bowl.

But come sunset and the action hotted up.

Edna and Matilda put on long black robes, grey veils which had the effect of giving their faces a ghost-like appearance, then inspecting me who was wearing the same black suit I'd worn at Edith's funeral.

'You look very nice, dear,' Edna commented. 'Doesn't he, Matilda?'

Matilda nodded. At least I think she did. It was hard to tell what she was doing under that veil. 'Yes. But I think he looks more handsome with his hair brushed back. Parted he reminds me of that assistant in the shoe shop who once laid a familiar hand on Edith's ankle.'

Then all three of us sat in the lounge exchanging small talk while waiting for the sun to set. Aunt Edna said she had not known such warm weather since dear Mary-Lou *moved*, and Aunt Matilda expressed a hope that the threatened rain would hold off until Edith was nicely settled.

Presently I got tired of sitting and listening to their old voices and after excusing myself wandered out into the garden. Two young lads who had been keeping watch over the back wall, dropped out of sight while one shouted: 'He's got his funeral suit on! It must be tonight!' Shortly afterwards I heard a vast amount of door shutting and the locking of windows.

I looked upon a glorious sunset, but even as I watched little fat black clouds came drifting in from the east and set about demolishing that lovely scene, warning all who could read the message that night would soon position its platoons in both city and countryside.

Aunt Edna called from the kitchen doorway:

'Soon be time, David dear,' and indeed it was time to go indoors and face the horrors of unreality.

Both sisters had donned something more than a long black robe and a grey veil. A complete new personality that hinted at an odd kind of professionalism. I cannot, try as I may, explain how this was so, save I had the impression they were drawing upon an enormous fund of experience, that normally would be locked away in some dark recess of their brains.

I was pushed gently into the hall and made to face the stairs; Edna to my left and Matilda to my right. Both looked up the stairs with a kind of pathetic expectancy, before Edna called out in a quavering voice:

'It's time, Edith dear. It's your *moving* time.'

I waited, not really expecting anything particular to happen, but right deep down knowing it would.

Edith's bedroom door creaked open. The creaking was very drawn out as though someone with not too much strength to spare was pulling the door open very slowly.

The creaking stopped. The heavy footsteps began.

Edith-sized in granite – those were the words that flashed across my brain. Thump-thump-thump. The ceiling below must have trembled and possibly sent down a little shower of plaster. Very, very heavy footsteps that moved very, very slowly. They came out even more slowly on to the landing – and Edith emerged into view.

My first impression – white – white – white – with black pupilless eyes that moved. Moved all the time. I think there may have been a tiny spot of light dead centre, but I can't swear to that, for I was not just frightened – I was one babbling mass of trembling, trouser-pissing, stomach-heaving terror. That thing – Edith – she – it – was white plastic marble. Take a statue of a woman in a long white robe, then give it movement, but with no expression on the face at all, save for those moving black eyes, and maybe the merest suggestion of a smile etched round the mouth – and you may –

just may have some inkling of what that apparition looked like.

Only it was no apparition, or if it was, a damned solid one.

One dead white hand gripped the banister rail, then thump-thump down the stairs, with the two sisters shouting encouragement.

'Come on, Edith dear ... that's right ... don't worry about chipping the paint, David can put that right tomorrow morning. Pick your feet up, won't do to have you tumbling down like Cousin Jane did.'

She thumped-thumped down those stairs and as she came nearer I began to notice little details, like the tiny mole under her left eye, only now it too was dead white, and the rather nice lock of hair that used to dangle over her forehead; now it really did looked like brilliantly carved marble. And – yes – it did seem as if the ghost of a smile was etched round her mouth.

I had the impression it took quite an effort to step down into the hall, for she took some time to lower the left bare foot on to the fitted carpet, then hung on to the banister rail while she brought the right down to join it.

In fact I believe some kind of restorative – not rest – non-action was required, a standing still interval, when the only movement was continuously rolling black, pupilless eyes.

Presently Edna nudged me. 'David! What are you thinking about, dear? Give your Auntie Edith a nice kiss.'

God of my fathers – forgive me and save at least a remnant of my sanity – I BLOODY WELL DID IT. I kissed that cold horror and MY LIPS STUCK TO HER CHEEK. She was so cold my lips froze on contact and I left a strip of flesh behind when I pulled my mouth free. The two sisters looked at me reproachfully and Edna pushed a wad of tissues into my hand with a muttered: 'Blood on the carpet!' then wiped what I had left behind from Edith's cheek. You know, even in the midst of that body and brain numbing terror I still felt that I had blotted my copybook for kissing Aunt Edith too hard and messing up the hall carpet.

Edith went into action again. Very slowly along the hall, a careful walk over the front doorstep, then down the garden path to the front gate. We lined up on the pavement.

Edith in front. She was the pace setter. Edna next. Then Matilda with me bringing up a very reluctant rear. As we progressed down the High Street a gurgling scream came from a window over the butcher's shop, before a bright red curtain quivered and fell away, as though some falling body were clinging to it.

Matilda shook her head sadly. 'Peepers weepers. There's always one who just won't learn.'

After a while, when I had recovered sufficiently to think of something other than my own terror, I noticed that out here in the open Edith shone. Or glimmered whitely. When the moon slid behind a cloud bank she positively glowed. Like illuminated snow.

But she did look fearsome. I could well understand that someone who wasn't family and had not been acclimatized by degrees, giving vent to a howling scream just prior to slipping down into the pit of madness.

The cats on the Giant's Grave were letting rip now and the dogs seemed determined not to be outdone, and believe you me there is no sound more hideous on this earth than the united howls of a hundred or more cats and dogs.

We left the village behind and Edna and Matilda began to sing 'Home Sweet Home' and the way they sang it, I could hardly tell the difference between their din and that made by the cats and dogs.

The churchyard lane was full of potholes and I wondered what would happen if Edith were to stumble and fall flat on her white cold face, but fortunately that did not happen, although I almost knocked Matilda over when I tripped on a ruddy great stone.

We moved into the churchyard and eventually came to the mound of earth that covered all that I recognized as Edith's earthly remains.

Now comes the awful part.

Edith stood beside her grave and stared at the old church, rolling those dreadful black eyes and rather giving the impression she wasn't all that keen about doing whatever came next. Edna whispered, 'You move in, dear. Can't leave you standing here. The locals just wouldn't understand. And when the sun comes up, dear, you'll catch your death of heat.'

I shook my head quite violently when Matilda said to me, 'Can't you give your Auntie Edith a little shove, dear? That's all she needs to get her going.'

But Edith at length got herself going. Trod into the loose soil, pounded it down and ploughed her way up and in until she stood on the very peak of the mound, her feet covered with earth, her eyes rolling like black marbles.

The sisters expressed encouragement by clapping black-gloved hands together and saying, 'Well done, dear. Oh, very well done.' Then: 'Down you go, dear. Down you go.'

Grand-Aunt Edith began to vaporize.

She did. She did.

First the head began to dissolve into white, seething vapour. Then the neck went all floppy before running into the torso. After that the process speeded up. Arms sort of exploded into vapour, only there wasn't any sound. Torso collapsed, Vapour dropped around the legs as if to hide them from vulgar gaze. Then the entire mess sank into the grave and disappeared from view.

Edith had finally *moved*.

The two sisters lowered their heads and called out in low sweet voices: 'Bye-bye, dear. See you on Sunday.'

I can't be sure but I think that's the way vampires are born, but for what now passes for my peace of mind I'm not suggesting that Great-Aunt Edith became a vampire. If she had I am certain someone in the village would have mentioned it.

Before we left the churchyard, the moon being by now quite bright, they insisted we visit my empty plot. My grave to be. Edna looked at it, while Matilda looked at me. I think they both spoke together.

'To think that one day you will *move* into here! How thrilled you must be.'

But the final chilly twist came on the way home. We all three walked abreast. Edna on my left, Matilda to my right. Suddenly Edna looked back and expelled her breath as a deep sigh of annoyance.

'It is really too bad,' she said.

I looked back. A column of vapour about five feet six high was drifting down the middle of the road. Matilda stamped her foot.

'No, dear, not until Sunday. You really mustn't follow us. Go back.'

Both sisters advanced towards the column making shooing sounds.

I ran towards the railway station.

OK, I passed up two hundred thousand pounds, but money is not everything.

IV

Element of Doubt

A.L. Barker

'By the by,' said Hopcraft, fidgeting before getting up to go, 'what about Midgeley's paper?'
'What indeed.'
'You have it, I presume?'
'It is in my possession, yes. How much do you know of it?'
'Nothing. Midgeley spoke once of possibilities undreamed of, I was going through a bad bout of insomnia at the time and any dreams would have been welcome.'
'I doubt if Midgeley's are dreamable.'
'He hinted at profound implications.'
'He was certainly in over his head. I'm not questioning his intellectual stature, which we know was considerable. But I fear that in his last illness he was in an incendiary situation, febrile and possibly hallucinatory. He was over-reaching.'
'In what direction?'
'I can only describe it as a leap in the dark, accompanied by the sort of hyperbole no scientist should adopt. Speculation merely.'
'He was a reliable worker in the field. I would not expect him to cut corners.'
'His last exercise seems to me like a try for a raison d'être.'
'There is an element of doubt?'
'You could say that.'
'I take it you will not refer to his paper?'
'It would only diminish his reputation. But let me read it to you.'
Hopcraft looked at his watch. 'Not now, I have a meeting with the dean. Send me a transcript.'

When Hopcraft had gone, Irving set about putting the pages of his contribution to the Cardew memorial lectures in order. He had typed them here on the College machine because of trouble with the line-hold on his old portable at home.

His piece was sound and predictable, he wasn't breaking new ground. To be honest, which he hoped he was, he found himself without any new ground. It was a recurrent situation and one had to conceal it, for one's own good and that of the establishment.

Midgeley's paper was in fact not here in college, but safely at home. There was something *un*safe about it, a veiled general threat which Irving felt he should analyse. If analysis was possible. He was conscious of a marked reluctance to read it again.

Irving placed the tips of his fingers together in a thoughtful gesture and intoned: 'It is an honour to be invited to contribute to these memorial lectures –' No, better be casual, some people would be aggrieved at not being invited. He stood up, plunged both hands in his pockets and stooped smilingly as to an audience of friends. 'This isn't the first time I've contributed to the Cardew lectures, but it's still a great occasion for me. Tonight I want to talk about the proliferation principle.'

A nicely non-committal subject which would take him a long way without the obligation to arrive. It was open to question – this too was a recurrent situation – whether there was anywhere to arrive. He lacked Midgeley's faith. Midgeley had held to his belief that there was an Answer. And at the end, believed he had found it.

Irving had known him from their schooldays. As a child, underendowed, Midgeley cried 'Why?' when other boys punched him, when his locker was rifled, his trousers torn off him. It was the need to know exceeding his distress. At the end it had exceeded his reason.

Irving wadded his lecture notes into his overcoat pocket and went home.

*

In theory his children waited up to say goodnight to him. In practice it was Alice, the nursegirl, who waited. Caspar and Candida were asleep, Caspar with his thumb in his mouth,

Candida crossly clutching her pillow. Alice sat on the nursery floor, surrounded by the children's toys. She was actually sitting on a pink and white rabbit and the rabbit's glass eye looked up from under her generous rump. She looked up at Irving, her eyelashes spiked black by an unskilled hand.

It had become a subject of mild amusement between Irving and his wife that the girl was besotted. She made no secret of it. In her early teens, plump, steamy and heavy-breathing, she breathed most heavily in Irving's presence. He had remarked, in her hearing, how draughty the house was become. She remained unaware that it was a joke at her expense.

She sat there now, on the rabbit, gazing at Irving and melting. She could be seen to melt, warm beads welled out of her pores and dried on her cheek like dew. Irving thought she must be the purest thing in the house, not excluding the children who were tarnished with his own genes.

He nodded to her, smiled, and kissed his unconscious son and daughter. It was what he had come to do, though something was due to the girl. She was waiting.

'Have they been good?' They hadn't, judging by Candida's scowl. He picked up an engine from the floor. One of the wheels fell off. 'Dear, dear –' Oxygenated, Alice half rose from the rabbit and for a second he feared she thought he was declaring himself. He hastily tossed the toy into the playbox. 'These things are inexcusably trashy.'

Her face was like a diagram face, without a single identifying mark, save for the blacked eyelashes. They, indeed, had congruity, as if they were the beginning of something else. Irving might have stayed to figure it out, but there were people coming to dinner.

'The Boldertons. They're new friends. I don't yet know if I like them. I certainly don't know if you would.' He was surprised to hear himself say, 'I can't ask you to join us.'

'You mustn't worry about me.'

He gave her a friendly wave as he went. But there was something in his hand – Caspar's broken engine.

*

'That girl takes too much on herself,' Irving's wife, Helen, said as they were undressing that night.

'On the contrary, she doesn't take on enough. Bolderton sees to that.'

'I'm talking about Alice.'

'The children's Alice?'

'Who else?'

'We weren't talking about her.'

'I was.'

'If you try to carry on a conversation we haven't been having, you must expect to be misunderstood.'

Irving spoke with asperity. He had just found a red rose hidden in his pyjama trousers. A thorn had scratched him on the inner tender part of his thigh. It could have been worse – the flower was wedged in the crotch of his trousers. It was a totally risible situation. He mustn't give Helen the chance to use it. He had noted a certain wryness in her smile and knew enough psychology to foresee that she might be sufficiently piqued to tell it as an after-dinner story.

He threw the rose under the bed, making a mental note to remove it in the morning. He could not think of a way of rebuking the girl without making himself look absurd.

'What has Alice taken on?'

'I don't altogether trust her. She's two-faced.'

Irving, checking his pyjama trousers for thorns, said vexedly, 'I don't find her even one-faced – she's totally forgettable.'

'I suppose it follows.'

'What follows what?'

'One or two faces or none. She plans to be an actress.'

'Oh lord.'

'She's working to pay for her training at RADA. I daresay she practises.'

'Practises?'

'Registering emotion.' Helen said gravely, 'Perhaps she practises on you.'

Next morning when Irving looked under the bed, the rose had gone.

It was his turn to walk the children. He took them to the common. They ran screeching towards the ponds and he settled himself on a wooden seat with a view of the Surrey hills.

Midgeley and Alice were mingled in his thoughts. It was a matter of contemporaneity. In all else, of course, they were poles apart, except perhaps in ardour. One might say they were both desirous, Midgeley of an open-and-shut theory, Alice of some fanciful but fleshly consummation ...

At that point Irving was obliged to get up and supervise his children who were making mud pies with their gloves on.

There were some fraught moments before he could take up his thoughts again, and then his thoughts took *him* up, by the scruff. He was vividly reminded of the last time he saw Midgeley.

Midgeley had sent for him, being by then confined to his bed. Irving found him still working, prematurely buried under books and papers. He was in a highly emotive state, exultant, frenetic and fearfully anxious. He babbled about a concept, not new – according to him it was as old as time and had been lying around under men's noses waiting to be noticed. Midgeley, it was obvious, believed that he was the unveiler of a universally important fact. It would, he said, 'equate the world'. Those were his words, but having spoken them, he was seized with feverish secrecy and scrambled all his papers out of sight under the bedclothes.

Irving, who was unaccustomed to illness, was surprised at the change in this unremarkable man. There was a weird brilliance about him, an apostolic fervour. Irving was irreligious and found it quite unsettling.

Midgeley planned to deliver his theory to the world as a Cardew lecture, forgetting or overlooking the fact that he hadn't been asked to speak. In the event of his indisposition preventing him from speaking, he wished to make Irving his executor. Irving would have been willing, had there been anything to execute. He had questioned Midgeley patiently until Midgeley had some sort of seizure and Irving had to leave. Next day Midgeley died. His paper was delivered to Irving by special messenger.

Irving had studied it with curiosity and increasing dismay. It was a mish-mash of science, theology and cloud-cuckoo. Midgeley's proposition, if it could be so called, was that good and evil exist in equal doles, issued to mankind for general consumption. Like two pieces of soap, thought Irving incredulously, soluble like soap – the implication being that in due time the supply would be used up and since good and evil could only exist in relation to each other there would be no occasion for sin, and Man would return to his first state of innocence. There was some quasi-religious affiliation with a nuclear apocalypse – a sort of Big Wash, perhaps, to dispose of all the soap in one go.

Irving's pity was tinged with envy. Midgeley had found his Answer and, so to speak, gone off with it. Whether it was valid or not was immaterial.

There were times when Irving thought that the equation would never come out anyway. Let x equal a, equal z, equal any old thing, the quantities weren't merely unknown, they were incompatible.

But he got a shock, an unpleasant twinge, when he went into his study after lunch and found Midgeley's paper on his desk. Set fair and square in the centre, the damn silly title – 'Return to Eden' – scrawled across the front page.

Irving had locked it away in the bottom drawer. The drawer was still locked and the key on his key-ring. His own lecture notes, which he had left on his typewriter, had vanished.

Helen, as might be expected, knew nothing about it. He asked her, simply to ratify a doubt more than anything else. He *must* be mistaken and needed to hear her say so.

'You put the wrong ones away,' she said obligingly. 'It's easily done, one heap of paper looks much like another.'

'Not when one is in Midgeley's handwriting.'

'You've been working on it, haven't you?'

'Why should I be?'

'Aren't you going to read it at the Cardew?'

'Only if I want to make a laughing-stock of myself and of the faculty.'

'I thought he was your friend.'

'He was. But if I tell you that he was trying to apply the quantum theory to infinities –'

'I should be no wiser.'

'It's *my* paper I'm concerned about!'

'Don't shout.'

'Where is it?'

'I have no idea.'

'For God's sake! I'm due to read it this evening —'

He ransacked his study. Panicking, he ran downstairs and went through his overcoat. He turned out pocket linings, opened and shook the umbrellas in the hallstand, flung everything off the hooks, including the children's coats. The children ... He was snatching at straws. Reasoning would come later, if at all.

In the nursery he surprised a scene of simple charm. Caspar and Candida were kneeling at Alice's feet and she was reading them a story. She paused at sight of Irving. The children gave him one glance and clamoured for her to go on.

She smiled dreamily at Irving. 'When the prince came to where Beauty lay sleeping, he placed a single red rose on her bosom and stooped to wake her with a kiss —'

'Not that!' cried Caspar. 'Tell about the gingerbread house.'

'Gingerbread — ugh!' said Candida. 'It was a coffee fudge house with a lemon meringue roof — I'd eat that first.'

'You couldn't reach the roof!'

'Naturally it was a little tiny house —'

'Have either of you been into my study?' said Irving.

Caspar shook his head. Candida, who overworked a word once she had learned it, said, 'Naturally not.'

Irving looked at Alice. 'You — what about you?' She blinked those ridiculous eye-lashes of hers, like spent match-sticks. 'Have you been into my study for any reason? Any reason at all?' She continued to gaze at him, though with what in mind he couldn't tell. 'Or for no reason? I want the truth!'

The children were wishing him to go away. Candida actually attempted to dismiss him. 'The witch put Hansel in a cage and poked him to see if he was fat enough for the oven —'

'Listen to me!' Irving, standing over them, spoke through his teeth. 'Some very important papers have disappeared from my study. I left them on top of the typewriter. If you know anything about them and own up now, I won't be angry. I won't punish you.'

It flashed on him then that amorality could be what Alice and Midgeley had in common. It was, after all, the logical outcome of Midgeley's theory — a world without sin or virtue, and Alice's face, when one came to study it, as he was now, was not innocent, so much as uncommitted.

He felt that he was the victim of some sort of ridiculous conspiracy. He shouted over their heads, to the conspirator, 'Where the hell are my notes!'

Candida, who was bored, started a howl of convenience, the ploy of hers which invariably paid off. She could work up the decibels as confidently as any professional soprano.

'Candida, stop that noise!'

Helen had come into the room. She carried a sheaf of papers which she thrust at Irving. 'Is this what you're looking for?'

'My notes!'

'They've been flying round the kitchen.'

'Flying?'

'Like birds.'

Irving leafed through the sheets. They were out of order, but complete. 'If this is a joke, I hope it's over.'

'I hope so. And done with.'

'That's for me to say.'

'Meaning?'

'It was stupid and inconsiderate.' Irving's voice rose. 'It was a bloody fool thing –'

'Not in front of the children, please.' Helen turned and went.

Irving ran downstairs after her. 'Have you any idea of the work I put into this?'

In the kitchen she faced him. She was white and very tense. 'You told me it was a rehash of one of your course lectures.'

'That's still a hell of a lot of work. Am I to understand you took it to wrap the potato peelings?'

'I promise you I never laid a finger on your notes until they ended up at my feet.'

Irving smiled unpleasantly. 'Having flown in through the window? I think you said they were flying.'

Helen groped for a chair and sat down. 'I came into the kitchen and there they were. I thought that a lot of birds had got in –'

'Birds?'

'They were like seagulls – circling.'

'Are we talking about the same thing?'

'Sheets of paper flying round and round. So quiet – stealthy – horrid!'

She was genuinely upset. Irving said crisply, 'The effect of some sort of updraught. A current of air.'

'The windows were shut. There was no air!'

'The question is, how did my notes get out of my study and into the kitchen?'

'I don't know!'

'They flew in, of course!'

They stared at each other. Irving had no difficulty identifying Helen's thoughts. She knew she was being absurd and she was angry with herself, and with him for being unsympathetic. He took her hand.

She snatched it away. 'There's something else –' She pointed across the room.

In a far corner, lying on its side on the floor, was a huge earthenware crock. It was unbroken, but the bags of flour that had been in it had burst, scattering their contents over a wide radius.

'What happened?'

'It missed me by inches,' said Helen.

'You hadn't put it securely on the shelf –'

'It flew at me!'

'*Flew?*'

'I could have been killed!'

'My dear, you have had a couple of minor but annoying accidents –'

'It flew off the shelf and didn't break!'

'It will certainly have cracked, but I agree it appears whole *in situ* –'

Irving approached the crock. Before he reached it, it started to roll gently to and fro.

Helen gasped. Irving hesitated. The thing was plainly unbroken and appeared to be demonstrating the fact. He seized it by its neck and set it upright. 'Vibration.'

'What vibration?'

'Possibly from the M 20.'

'The M 20 is miles away.'

'Or the fridge or the freezer.'

They stood listening. The kitchen, usually cosy with the working hum of domestic appliances, was stolidly silent. 'You see?' said Irving. 'It's really nothing.'

'Where are the birds?' Candida appeared in the doorway.
'Birds?'
'You said there were birds in the kitchen. I want to see them.'
'There are no birds.'
'You said!'
'It was a figure of speech,' said Helen.
Candida glared. 'Why do you say there are things if there aren't?'

Irving told Helen, 'I leave you to answer that one,' and went to his study. Midgeley's paper still reposed on his desk. He took it up and leafed through page after page of Midgeley's execrable handwriting. He secured it with a bulldog clip and put it in the bottom drawer of his desk. He had difficulty locking the drawer, somehow the key had become slightly bent.

He was spreading out his own notes and was starting to reassemble them in numerical order when he heard a scream followed by a rumble as of shifting heavy furniture.

As he ran into the hall, Helen came from the kitchen. Her eyes were wild, she had Candida by the shoulders, pushing the child before her.

'What is it? What's wrong?'

Helen could not speak, she was sobbing in her throat. Irving tried to touch her, she fought him off.

'For Heaven's sake –'

She spread her arms about the child, shielding her – Helen, his wife, shielding his child from him.

'Tell me what's happening!'
'The knife –'
'What knife?'
'The carving knife – it came straight at Candida!'
'Came?'
'Out of the air!'

Irving's heart sank. He was up against something which could not be wished away. Something in Helen, his calm, temperate, rational wife.

'Come, let's go and sit down. I'll get you something to drink –'

'It's there I tell you! Sticking in the table!'

He went into the kitchen, came back, trying to smile. 'There's nothing.'
'But the knife –'
'Is in the dresser drawer. Where it always is.'
'The table –'
'Is unmarked.'
'The table moved – came after us!'
'My dear –'
'Can I do anything?'
Alice and Caspar had come downstairs, Alice holding Caspar's hand. Helen cried out like an animal and snatched Caspar away.
'Just a small mishap,' said Irving.
'Small mishap? My children's lives are in danger!'
'Candida,' Irving stooped to look into his daughter's eyes, 'what did you see?'
'I didn't see the birds.'
'Did you see anything?'
'I didn't!' Candida stamped her foot.
Caspar started to whimper. Irving said to Alice, 'Take them upstairs.'
Helen, very white, held both children to her. 'They are never to go near that girl again.'
'Helen!'
'I'm taking them away and I shan't bring them back until she's out of the house!'
'What has Alice to do with it?'
'Everything!'
'For Heaven's sake, pull yourself together!'
Helen could be seen making the effort. Icy, but unsteady, she said, 'It's well known that this sort of thing can happen with adolescents.'
'What sort of thing?'
'Manifestations.'
'My dear –' Irving swallowed. A little pseudo-science was harder to take than sheer vagary. 'That's mere supposition. Nothing's been proved, or can be proved –'
'It's not safe for any of us. You too,' said Helen, bundling the children into their coats, 'should be warned. Get her out of the house tonight. I'm going to my parents.'

'To Winchester?'

'I'll ring you tomorrow to check that she's gone.'

'You haven't packed – This is sheer folly!'

'I have my car-keys and enough petrol to get us there. That's all that matters.' Helen threw her own coat over her shoulders. 'I won't risk another moment here.'

She didn't. The next moment they were gone. Gusts of rain blew in through the open front door. Irving stood waiting for the sound of Helen's car. He made no move to stop them. He knew that Helen right or Helen wrong, it was best to let them go.

Alice, of course, had heard it all. He sighed, so did she, though without regret. She was merely taking in air. Her bosom rose, replenished.

'I'm sorry,' he said. 'My wife is rather upset.'

'It wasn't me.'

'You mustn't blame yourself.'

She moved to close the door. 'I don't have to go, do I?'

'I'm afraid you do. Helen – You see, something happened which she associates with you.'

'Why?'

'There's a belief – a superstition – that certain happenings – disturbances – are activated by the physical presence of some-one your age. Someone who is growing up.' He was choosing his words. 'It's considered to be a difficult time.'

'I'd have felt something, wouldn't I?'

'I don't know.'

'Why couldn't it be her? She could be having a difficult time.'

It was a distinct possibility – the only one, so far as he could see. Helen was approaching the other difficult age of woman, the change of life – and sometimes of personality.

'I think you must go and pack your things.'

Alice sighed, this time with regret. 'I like it here.'

'I'm sorry.'

'Will you come and see me when I'm on the stage? I'm going to be an actress.'

'I know.'

'I'm going to be famous.' She sighed again, as if it would be a chore. 'I'll do all the big parts, St Joan, Rebecca, Hedda Gabler.'

Irving thought how provident she was being by despising

what she hadn't got and might never get. Insuring against failure. He knew now what the matchstick eyelashes were the beginning of: make-up. She would need layers of it to make her up to St Joan, Rebecca, Hedda Gabler.

Then she said, 'The evil that men do lives after them, the good is often buried with their bones.'

'What?'

'It's Shakespeare.'

'But why say it?'

'Why not? I know lots of Shakespeare.'

It was Irving's turn to gaze. She had just shot a cherished proposition to pieces. The words made nonsense of Midgeley's paper. If they were to be believed, mankind was damned.

But Midgeley's paper was nonsensical anyway, and Irving certainly had not cherished it. He said, smiling, 'Shakespeare could be wrong, you know.' In a face as young as hers it was possible to see into every pore without distaste. He was moved to touch a finger to her cheek. 'He was wrong about this too too solid flesh. It does melt.'

*

The Cardew lecture that evening was being moderately well attended. Hopcraft, as chairman, spoke briefly, acknowledging that Irving needed no introduction. Irving mounted the platform to a rustle of applause.

He plunged both hands in his pockets and stooped chummily towards his audience. 'This isn't the first time I've had the honour to contribute to this series of lectures. It's still a great and memorable occasion for me. Tonight I want to speak about the proliferation principle. I hope you may find something in my talk worth remembering –'

He hoped he wasn't smirking. He spread his notes on the lectern, glanced down at them. Glanced up, and down again. His smile fading, he gripped the lectern for support. He was seen to snatch up the sheets one by one, and one by one let them fall.

Hopcraft, on the platform with him, saw nothing amiss. The pages were neatly typed. On one which had fluttered down by his feet, he noted the title, 'Return to Eden'. It suffered from a dropped lower case 'e', a peculiarity of Irving's machine.

V

The Manse

J.C. Trewin

1

The pony-trap, a Cornish jingle, clopped off from the station at Polruth into the clinging autumn darkness. We took a road towards the moor, or barren heath, that lay like a rug over the extreme heel of southern Cornwall.

'Glad you've come to us, Mr Treleaven,' said Wilfred, the driver, as we were lost in the November evening; at that hour it could have been anywhere in the deep country. 'King Edward, too, and Queen Alexandra out at the Mount.'

'We're not likely to meet,' I said cheerfully. 'All I'm looking for is a month of peace.'

'You'll get that all right at the Manse. It's my belief you're Miss Mary's first visitor ... Hoop, boy! He feels the weight of that trunk.'

'My typewriter,' I said. Wilfred chuckled: 'Pen and ink for me.'

The bay pony began to trot along a by-road. 'Who gave 'ee the word, then?' Wilfred asked. 'Not Lawyer Hallett?'

'Of Four Crossings. Yes. He's known me since a boy. I lived out at Manaccan, remember.'

'Oh, we know about 'ee in St Loe, Mr Treleaven. Not that we've read your books, mind, but we're happy you've come. You wouldn't have set foot in the Manse a year ago in old Benjamin's time ... Minister for forty years and always his own master ... Best get up your coat-collar. This is where the blast comes.'

Indeed, a full wind whipped across the exposed moor. Not a

star glimmered; no light anywhere except the faint glow of the jingle's oil-lamp. Then presently, as the wheels rattled down a stony slope, I saw beneath, in a deep cup of the moor, the scattered gleams of St Loe village. It was years since I'd been anywhere near it, but memory had suggested that it was the perfect place to work unworried, and Ted Hallett had confirmed this. 'Mary Rundle needs visitors,' he had written. 'You'll be doing her a good turn if you go there.' So here I was; I wanted nothing more than to be on my own for a few weeks to put things together. No distractions; easy sleep by night; by day head-down at the desk and a walk or two in what used to be my own country, or close to it. No friends to stop me concentrating, and concentration just now was essential. I could do without books; all the papers were in my trunk, something the tireless pony would be glad to throw off.

'Old Benjamin, yes,' Wilfred went on, seeming to talk in rhythm to the gentle bouncing of the jingle. 'Benjamin Leonard. Dr Leonard – doctor of philosophy. Strange old man. Eighty-two when he died, twelve months back.'

'I know that I heard of him, but very vaguely. Did he own the manse?'

'He did. No chapel now in the village. Benjamin owned that too, what remained of it –'

'Remained?'

'That's the word. He had his bad years. Very bad years but nothing stopped him in his work. A reading man, a clever man, for all his fixed notions. There were things he wouldn't have and he preached against them, all hell-fire, on Sundays. Card players, racing men, every hate you'd expect, Mr Treleaven, in what he called the devil's net. But first of all he hated actors, the pomping folk. A fanatic he was; something must have happened far back before he moved down to us. He preached against actors from his very first day.'

I was puzzled. 'But surely they stay only three years in one chapel, six at most. I've got two uncles in the ministry. And you say he was here for forty years?'

'That's right, Mr Treleaven. We're the smallest place. Congregations slipped away. Some getting old; some not liking him. Nobody would take the pulpit. It suited him to stay on, and it suited the planners. Ben had a fair bit of money, and when the chapel was nigh empty, all going across to Pralla on a Sunday, he bought the whole property. His wife had died, poor soul. And then – well, 'twas a judgment on him, I'd say – his daughter, Miss Ellen, ran off with an actor. Broke his heart.'

'An actor, Wilfred? Here?'

'Aye. They get about. Mary Rundle will tell 'ee ... But don't fret, Mr Treleaven; she won't talk unless you ask her straight. She kept house for Ben through more 'n thirty years, bore with his ways as faithful as you'd wish, and they wanted some bearing with. She's a lonely soul now; it's wise for her to take lodgers, somebody round the house, though she's been a time coming to it.'

We turned a sharp corner. 'Here's the manse, Mr Treleaven. I'll set down your trunk. Whoa, my pretty!'

The jingle had stopped outside a house I could barely see in the gloom. But there was a wavering glow through its fanlight. A chain rattled, a door creaked open, and inside, holding an oil-lamp askew, was an elderly woman in a black dress. She greeted me in a plaintive voice, genteel enough though I could sense the country tone beneath it. 'Come in, Mr Treleaven. I've been waiting. Bring that trunk in, Wilfred, would you. Leave it in the hall.'

When he shouldered it into the narrow passage as if it were a bundle of feathers, he turned to her: 'Mind your lamp, Mary.' He took it and placed it on a bracket beneath a bristle of empty coat-hangers. 'Chimney's smoked. That could be dangerous. Fire's fire.'

'I've every cause to know' she said with unexpected spirit. 'Well, you'd best pay Wilfred, Mr Treleaven. I've supper on the table.'

'Five shillings,' Wilfred said. 'We'll meet tomorrow, Mr Treleaven. See me down shop.' He whispered behind his cupped hand. 'And tell me what you see and hear.'

I began to wonder where I had come. The jingle slipped away. Miss Mary took the lamp and lighted me through the passage she had glorified as a hall, single doors to right and left, a stair climbing steeply on the right. 'I've laid in the kitchen. Do you eat first, Mr Treleaven, or do you go upstairs?'

'I'd better get my trunk up,' I said.

'Please yourself then. I'll follow. You're at the landing, Dr Benjamin's old room. There's hot water in the jug by the washstand.'

I hauled the trunk up, scraping it more than once, and guiltily, against the linoleum, while Miss Mary followed with her lamp, still wavering a little. At the top, though the stairs bent round to another flight, as steep as the first, I opened the bedroom door into what seemed to be a small library. There were certainly a bed, a miniature table by it, a chair, and a washstand with flowered china bowl and soap-dish, but the walls were thick with bookshelves and what looked to me like rubbed half-calf bindings, though it was impossible to tell. I could see even less after Miss Mary – clumsily, I thought – had lit the tiny egg-shaped lamp on the bed-table and pattered downstairs. All this must be for the morning.

I washed, threw back the lid of the trunk, put my pyjamas on the bed, and stumbled down the stairs which had no hand-rail and (I decided) must be nearly perpendicular. It was certainly more cheerful in the kitchen where Miss Mary waited for me with a cold pasty, a not very successful treacle sponge, and the strongest tea I could remember.

Mary Rundle was probably about sixty, stooping a little, with iron-grey hair and dark eyes that struck me then as curiously frightened, as if she could see something beyond my shoulder and that something was watching us. Tonight she had not much to say. My study, a word she emphasised, for obviously it meant a lot to her, would be on the ground floor, the first door off the hall. It used to be Benjamin's – she had dropped the Doctor – and there were many more of his books in it; he lived for nothing else. I would find it quiet to write. The village was very quiet, too much some people said. Yes, she would be glad of company herself; nobody had been with her since Benjamin died, or (a hasty correction) hardly anyone. She had kept house through thirty years and more since she had lost her mother; they lived up at Four Turnings and she had worked sometimes for Lawyer Hallett.

I tried to keep up a friendly chat, but it was difficult. This was the time in any new acquaintance when two people get to know each other, and it occurred to me that she was not particularly interested to know. She did ask politely what I was writing, and when I told her it was a life of Macready, this clearly conveyed nothing whatever. When I added 'an actor' she went very still; I supposed I should have kept it to myself, though goodness knew why. Anyway, an alarm clock on the table pointed to ten. 'Perhaps I had better go up now, Miss Mary?' I said. 'It was a fair journey from London, you know.'

She rose sharply. 'Breakfast at eight then, Mr Treleaven. If that will suit you.' She paused, and her semi-genteel tone slipped for a moment into dialect. 'If 'ee should hear anything in the night, take no heed. Old houses can sound it off, and we're noisier than most.'

'I sleep very well, Miss Mary. Goodnight.' She said no more but appeared to be listening for something, so I climbed that wretched stair – no light now in the passage – to a room that I felt was coldly cheerless in the flicker of its miniature brass lamp. This merely heightened the shadows about those loaded shelves. I did notice that one book had fallen out and was lying on the floor below the gap; picking it up, I glanced casually at the title before pushing it back. It was called *The Smoke of Their Torment*, printed by the Masters of Revelation, with some Cornish town – Padstow, I believed – following the name. The author was Benjamin Leonard, PhD, and the same name was on the fly-leaf in a scholarly italic hand, St Loe, 1875.

The feather bed was comfortable enough, though I had never been a man for feathers, and soon enough I was asleep, for how long I had no notion. In the bleaker small hours – it must have been – I woke suddenly in the thickest darkness which seems to be darker when any place is strange. My lamp had gone out, and there was a lingering smeech of oil. Not a gleam beyond the window-square. I was conscious only that somebody was moving stealthily across the floor to the further bookshelves. The visitor, whoever it was, appeared to be lame; there was a perceptible dragging of one foot. I attempted to speak, but at such moments as these when one is scarcely awake, words dry in the throat. I lay very still while the faint steps receded, the door clicked shut, I heard a slow padding on the stair, and at length the clinking of the front-door chain.

By now I was fully awake. Fumbling for matches and upsetting the box, nearly empty anyway, I managed with some trouble to light the tiny lamp which appeared to be almost out of oil. It was just burning up thinly under its glass shade when the sound of singing rose suddenly from not very far off. It was a simple hymn tune, but the singing, unaccompanied, was far from confident; there could not have been more than half-a-dozen voices. I caught words which were unfamiliar to me (and not very helpful) even though I knew our hymn-book pretty well:

> Pray now that in this nation
> We may be saved from sin,
> From evil desecration
> That injures all within;
> From falsehoods that will lead us
> Where fires are burning high,
> Where not a soul will need us
> As miserably we die.

The singing stopped, as if it had been cut off. A male voice began to speak, an angry, insistent, grating tone from which I got nothing except a single phrase, 'And the smoke of their torment ascendeth up for ever and ever,' then a deadly silence.

2

For a while I was utterly still, awake and every sense alert. But sleep conquered, and when I did open my eyes I saw that daylight was vague beyond the rucked muslin curtains of the small window; somewhere rooks were cawing with deplorable enthusiasm. I must have knocked over the lamp; it lay on its side in a pool of oil. The room was intolerably stuffy, and the window would not open. Washing and dressing as quickly as I could, I glanced round at the closely-packed bookshelves filled with titles that were scarcely encouraging: *The Number of the Beast, Babylon and the Abominations of the Earth, The Pillar of Salt: Collected Sermons*. Then I saw that the book I had replaced last night – or had I? it seemed so long ago – *The Smoke of Their Torment*, was missing; nothing lay beneath the gap. A knock:

Mary was calling to me, a shade petulantly: 'Your breakfast, Mr Treleaven. It's gone eight.'

She waited for me in the kitchen, still in her black dress, now with a small black apron. As she put a porridge-bowl on the table, she asked only a single question: 'The bed suited?'

'Nothing wrong with the bed, Miss Mary. But I had a trying dream.' She listened without speaking, but I noticed the curious fear in her eyes.

'Did you hear anything?' I asked.

'I hear a good deal, Mr Treleaven, but it makes little sense to me.'

She did not comment, merely pursed her lips, when I told her that the bedside lamp had been knocked over. After breakfast she took me to the room at the front of the house that was to be my study and had been Benjamin Leonard's. It might have been a replica of the bedroom except that it had neither bed nor washstand but an old desk, its leather top scored with many scratches. The shelves were crowded with books that I had no particular urge to open.

Quickly I set out my bundled papers and the heavy typewriter at which Mary stared as if it were the instrument of torture that no doubt it was.

'I'd better go out for a bit before starting work,' I said feebly.

Five minutes later I was in the cold, windy road – one could hardly call it a street – and facing the manse, a stark three-storeyed house uncompromisingly bare, in stock brick. No sign of a garden, and I didn't think there could be one at the back.

What did strike me was the shell of a building of some size, about seventy to a hundred yards away. It looked like a chapel that had been burnt out, and indeed it had been: a rectangle of scorched walls, two big round-headed windows, a pediment. Within, an empty space. Though I presumed that there had been a gallery, there was no longer anything to show. The floor had been destroyed, but planks made a bridge across it. All was swept and very still. Clearly this has been Benjamin's chapel where he had thundered across the years. I shivered a little and walked away towards the village, observing as I passed the manse that Mary Rundle was staring out at me through the study's smudged glass.

Nobody seemed to be abroad, anywhere. St Loe was hazily

The Manse

as I recalled it, sheltered on all sides by the slopes of the moor and suggesting that it had been dug out laboriously long ago. Oddly, I had forgotten that there was a chapel, but my aunt, who was a dedicated class-leader at Manaccan where I had stayed with her so often, used to say that St Loe was outside the circuit now, though she never explained why. The hamlet could have been a calm, orderly republic. Its cottages, mostly shadowed by elms – one of these held the active rookery – resembled the prints that illustrated ancient books of simplified rustic legend and could have been interchanged without anyone knowing the difference.

Surprisingly (if I had not known it already) there was no pub, only one shop – owned by Wilfred's family, I thought, from the beginning of time – and, as far as I had been aware, no school: the children, not many of them, walked every morning up to Four Turnings and over the Far Fields to Pralla. Unexpectedly I did pass a miniature village hall which looked coyly as if it had never been open, and could have been there simply on show. Still it must have been used because a handwritten poster, months old, continued to announce that 'the children' would be giving a performance of *Mrs Jarley's Waxworks*. Having once been an expert in this, at the age of ten, a superb Nelson with telescope and eye-patch, I did wonder a shade wistfully what the latest company could have been like.

I walked out from the houses – a group of about twenty, with a few outlying farms – and to Four Turnings where Edward Hallett's house stood on the windy brow of the hill up from St Loe. It was just as well to let him know I had arrived, but I was out of luck: a starched and sophisticated maid, curious in those surroundings, told me that the family was away until the end of the week. Nothing remained except to go back; after all, I had to do the work I had come down for, so I turned aside after going for a few minutes to the high moor. From it this morning I could see the blur of the distant headland, The Rill, where Cornish watchers first reported the sails of the Armada, Medina Sidonia's galleons bearing up from the south. Not a soul was walking the moor, though a van from Polruth did loiter by me, pulled by a veteran horse so tired of the whole business that its driver let it amble along as if they had days before them; perhaps they had. Presently they disappeared down the hill to St Loe, the cans of paraffin banging together at the back and making the same noise I remembered from my days at Manaccan.

I followed the van and wandered back through the hamlet, by the gentle, insignificant brook that trailed beside the road. Wilfred's shop was open. Standing alone among flour-bags, saucepans, and a lumber of pots and packages, he greeted me warmly:

'How you doing then?'

I told him as briefly as I could, and he listened with a gravity I had not suspected.

'I feared as much, Mr Treleaven, though what's going on I can't say. Nobody can ... The fire? Yes, three years back, a blaze in the night, nothing to be done. Ben swore it was a judgment on the village; his congregation had been leaving him Sunday by Sunday, walking to Pralla across the Far Fields; those too old for roaming had no more stomach for him. You should have heard what he said about those children in the waxworks. Yet he went on: two sermons every Sunday, eleven and six-thirty, good enough if you could get out before he began to talk. He wrote his books through the week. On Sundays he sang his own hymns, "Where fires are burning high", that sort of thing. Great man for fires, but melancholy-mad in the pulpit.'

'Where did he come from, Wilfred? Not from Meneage?'

'No, no, somewhere far up. Can't say what happened, but he came to us with a grudge against the world. Dear little wife; she died early. Then his daughter –'

'I know. Ran off with an actor. So you said. But how?'

'Little troupes would go round the Meneage villages, a night there, a night here. Ellen got in with a young man; I drove her once or twice, hoping Benjamin didn't know. Harmless stuff those players did, though Ben said the whore of Babylon was behind it all: that's not my religion, Mr Treleaven, and it's not yours. One night Ellen simply picked up her skirts and ran. That broke him for a time, but on a Sunday he was back, only a couple in the pews, and always poor Mary Rundle ... Well, are you staying on now you know all about us?'

'I shall be staying,' I said. 'I can write here, even if I'm sure Benjamin wouldn't have liked the book.'

'Actors in it?'

'Yes ... All about one man especially.'

'You'd better lose it, Mr Treleaven.' Wilfred was not smiling. 'And remember I shall be here if you want me. You may.'

I laid out my papers that afternoon at the back of Benjamin Leonard's desk and tried to get down to work: Macready had reached his first American tour. Nothing went smoothly. I couldn't fix my mind – on the whole, I believed, an orderly one – upon the events of sixty years ago which seemed incredibly remote. Instead, I looked at the two rather bad portraits over the far shelves: one, I presumed, of Benjamin himself in middle age, a sulky face and angry eyes above a stiff white cravat; another of a sad, sweet-faced woman who might have been his wife. There was no picture of the daughter Ellen, in the circumstances not surprising.

Miss Mary brought me tea, even stronger than it had been, at four o'clock. 'Not much progress,' I told her; 'I don't think the house likes me very much.' She noticed me shivering. 'It's a cold evening, Mr Treleaven. I'll get you a stove'; and she did, a big old-fashioned paraffin affair that smelt so strongly I hastened, when she was out of the room, to turn it down. What I was writing made little sense; it did seem, absurd though it was, that something or somebody was holding me back. I walked out in the twilight for ten minutes, nobody near, and I began to feel the want of company, even Miss Mary's, not a mistress of small talk.

As I re-entered the manse a reek of paraffin enveloped me. In the study the stove, which had been turned up to full, had been knocked over and was lying on its side red-hot and beginning already to burn a hole in the rug. I pulled it upright as best as I could and ran into the kitchen, meeting Mary who was carrying a lamp on a heavy stand of polished serpentine.

'What happened?' I cried.

She had no idea and looked as baffled as I felt. Bringing a cloth, she mopped up a pool of oil, I glanced at the desk and saw with horror that an ink-bottle had been emptied across my typescript. And by it, propped against the back of the desk, was Benjamin Leonard's book, *The Smoke of Their Torment*.

That evening we sat in the kitchen. Each of us knew, I think, what the other was anxious to say, and Mary spoke first, without warning.

'She should never have done it.'

'Who, Miss Mary?'

'Ellen. His daughter. She understood his ways and I begged her to think of him. But she was a teasy tripsy, Mr Treleaven, as obstinate as you'd find. Her mind was made up and she left us without so much as a goodbye. I thought he would never recover. Three days he was in his room, then he preached on the Sunday, a sermon that nobody that heard it – and there weren't many – would ever forget, an attack on the actors and all their ways. Ellen would write to him often; he wouldn't answer her, and I doubt if she expected it. He kept the letters for a while ... One day he put them in a pile on the fire and went out without looking back. The letters stopped ... Wait a moment!'

She was out of the room for five minutes. When she came back she was carrying the portrait of a brown-haired girl of twenty-one or two, something of a beauty, with her mother's gentle eyes but her father's firm-set mouth as well.

'You've seen the others in the study, Mr Treleaven. They were painted by a man who stayed hereabouts every year, over in lodgings at Pralla, and got to know Benjamin and his habits.'

'I wouldn't have thought –' (Should I call him Dr Leonard? Probably not.) 'I wouldn't have thought he'd have kept her picture ... Or, for that matter, sat for his own?'

'He pushed hers right away behind everything, but I was bent on keeping it ... His own picture, he said, was for the chapel's sake, a memory of him when he was gone.'

'But the chapel –?'

'Nobody knows, Mr Treleaven. It was in the middle of the night, a windy November. I woke to hear Benjamin, as he did often and often, padding down the stairs below me, dot-and-carry with his lame leg. The next thing I knew was waking again and hearing the noise of flames, a crackling noise, fearful if it's strange to you; when I got to the door it was worse. I slipped on my dressing-gown, ran down the two flights and into the road ... There it was, the chapel in a blaze. The wind, a "drummer" we call it here, had caught the fire and was fanning it up. Mercifully the other way from us.'

I could only ask the obvious question: 'How did it begin, Miss Mary?'

'Maybe the stove, a big one that Benjamin kept burning. It had fallen on its side – like yours in the study this afternoon – and it may have caught Benjamin's papers. For years he'd had them in great stacks behind a pew, philosophy and that, though I never saw him reading them ... Of course it might have been a tramp with a match; we've had tramps in St Loe, Mr Treleaven ...' Her voice trailed off; she did not believe what she was saying. 'Anyway, Benjamin accepted it as a sign. Fire was in his mind. Cleansing fires. Hell-fires. "Where fires are burning high" – that was his hymn; he'd write them by the score and expect us to know them. Oh yes, he went on preaching, but nobody would go back. I stuck by him, Mr Treleaven. It was frightening; you couldn't sit there unless you perched like a rook at the back. Not that he noticed. At home he was more and more careless. He'd spin round the lamp he was carrying as it might be the top of his walking-stick. Some say – Wilfred does – that on the night he died last November they saw fire in the sky, and I swear to hearing his last hymn. Coming out of nowhere.' She sang it half under her breath:

> Pray now to save our error
> In any evil path,
> For he that walks in terror
> Surrenders all he hath.

Clearly, I thought, listening to her, it would be ridiculous to stay. Yet to leave would be cowardly and selfish. Writing was out of the question. I asked Mary if I could stay with her through the evening, and there we spent the uneasy hours before supper and after, in the light of the lamp on its serpentine stand and with a desultory word now and again: Mary trying to knit and making a poor hand of it, and the 'drummer' wind, as she called it, which drove through the gap from Pralla, beating up against the panes. I stared at the broad sheets of a weekly paper without taking much in.

Something had to be said. 'Miss Mary,' I began, 'we both know what's happening in the house ... what may be happening. Shall I sit up tonight?'

There was a long pause.

' 'Twouldn't help, Mr Treleaven. When Benjamin's mind is set on something –' (and she spoke in the present tense) '– he'll carry it through. Best to go to our rooms, wait and watch.'

3

So at ten o'clock we rose. Frail and determined, she gave me my tiny lamp. 'Goodnight, my dear,' she said surprisingly. As she spoke, the big table lamp on its serpentine stand, neither of us within feet of it, tilted and crashed to the floor. She was trembling now. 'Get the broom from the scullery, if you please, Mr Treleaven' (we were back on the old terms). Rapidly, she swept up the glass from the broken chimney. 'No more we can do,' she said, and we went upstairs together, she to her room above me.

Even as strung up as I was, it was useless to fight off sleep. When I woke it could have been about one o'clock; wind was whipping round the house. Sheltered though St Loe was from most things, the 'drummer' could always find a way, and I remembered how the farmers had talked of it long ago. In a lull I heard, as I had done on the night before, footfalls limping across the room.

'Doctor Leonard!' I called huskily. 'Doctor Leonard!'

Heedless, the steps moved on. Again they went straight to the farther bookshelf, then I heard them retreating towards the door, followed by a metallic click of the latch and a muffled padding on the linoleum.

It was too much. For three minutes, perhaps, I could not stir. I managed to strike a match, but the bedside lamp (which I should never have extinguished) would not burn up: stupidly I found myself wondering whether the wick was clogged. Finally, thrusting on jacket and trousers, I got to the door.

From the top of the stairs I could see a clear line of bright light beneath the door of the study. At the same time a faint sound of singing drifted towards the manse, though the wind now was bearing away every word. I knew, and dreaded, that the grating, angry voice would follow, and it did, even if once more what it said was inaudible. Light had grown even brighter beneath the study door. I felt a touch on my arm; Miss Mary was beside me, half-dressed and with a plaid coat round her shoulders. She was shaking.

'It's Benjamin,' she whispered. 'What will he do now?' She looked down to the hall. 'But he has done it, Mr Treleaven ... The fire. His cleansing fire.'

'Come quickly, Miss Mary,' I said. We stumbled together into the hall, and as we passed the study door we could hear a crackle of flames. She half-clung to me. 'But that stove ... We never lit it again ...'

Outside, and in the glare of the rising, spreading fire, the drummer-wind was driving across St Loe. Somebody shouted my name. 'I was scared of this,' he panted. 'I was always scared. The jingle's here. Put Mary in it and give her my great-coat. You'll both be staying with me tonight.'

'Water, Wilfred! Can't we get water?'

'They'll have the alarm down to Pralla. But what could a couple of pails do to that? ... Lord! Just listen!' For a few moments Benjamin's hymn rose again, nearer now, a single, distorted, inhuman voice from the blazing manse:

> From falsehoods that will lead us
> Where fires are burning high ...

And, set sharply against the blaze, we saw for a bare moment a figure in a stiff white cravat. He held a calf-bound book and he appeared to be speaking; but a gust, sustained and furious, swept every syllable away.

Then only the fire remained.

VI

Waiting For A Bus

John Whitbourn

'Look out, it's Bob Springer – he's up at the bar!' I exclaimed.

'Avoid his eye and keep talking,' said Mr Disvan. 'There's quite a crowd in tonight and he may miss us.'

'Too late – he's seen me.'

'It's another late night for us then.'

'Don't bet on it.'

'Here he is.'

'Hello, Mr Disvan and Mr Oakley,' said our unwelcome guest. 'How are you?'

'Very well, thank you, Bob.'

'Would you like a drink, gentlemen?'

'Not if it obliges us to chaperon you home like the last time, thank you all the same.'

My pre-conceived, perhaps somewhat harsh response earned me one of Disvan's rare full-face stares. His expression was, as ever, inscrutable and the meaning of these admonitions or questions or whatever they were had to be guessed from the context of the occasion. In present circumstances I took it to signify some surprise on his part at my uncharacteristic lack of charity.

I'd observed before the surprising power of these visual shots across-the-bow upon the locals but was even more surprised to find an urgent desire to appease evoked in myself by the same means.

'I'm sorry, that wasn't really called for,' I said. 'It's just that ... well, I don't want to be late home tonight.'

'That's all right, I understand,' Springer said in a voice that was indeed full of sad understanding. 'Mind if I join you?'

'No, please do.'

He sat down and toyed absently with one of the empty beer bottles on the table.

'Of course,' he then said abruptly, 'Mr Disvan says I'm an old fool to live in such fear that I daren't walk home alone but then again, with all due respect, he's not had to suffer what I've suffered.'

'I think that that's irrelevant,' said Disvan.

'Many things in this world are irrelevant or illogical but are still powerful forces nevertheless,' replied Springer.

An attempt at profundity was the last thing I was expecting from a man of such surpassing anonimity and I felt a spark of revived interest in what he was obviously bursting to tell.

'That's very true,' I said.

Springer perhaps mistook interest for sympathy and turned to me as if to an ally.

'Mr Disvan says that, having been caught once, I'm in no further danger but that's easy for him to say and besides, how can he be sure?'

'Now, now, Bob,' said the man in question, 'you know me better than that. I don't say things for effect and I wouldn't state things of which I'm not sure.'

'No doubt what you say is true, Mr Disvan, but ... I can't help my fear.'

Successfully hooked at last I could not forbear to indulge my curiosity.

'Fear of whom?'

Springer looked at Disvan in a querying manner and he, by way of reply, merely shrugged. This seemed to answer whatever doubt held him back and the old man could then unload his burden.

'Fear of the person or thing that took forty years of my life.'

'Who was that?'

'I don't know.'

'You mean someone took forty years of your life but you don't know their name ...'

'No, he never told me it – not in all that time. But his name's not all that important.'

'No?'

'No, not really.'

'Well, how were all those years stolen from you?'
'By holding me captive so that the active years of my life passed me by and were wasted in nothingness.'
'That's very serious; who was responsible then – the state?'
'Certainly not, I've never, ever been in trouble with the law.'
'Some person did then ...'
'In a manner of speaking.'

I sighed, being somewhat exasperated, and tried another approach: 'Well, where were you held prisoner?'
'At the bus stop.'

My initial response was one of anger at being so obviously taken for a fool, but this was soon overridden by the transparent sincerity of the old man's face. Nevertheless my response was still rich with sarcasm:

'You were imprisoned for forty years at a bus stop, were you?'
'Not a bus stop but *the* bus stop on the way to my house – the one you walked me past the last time we drank together – but essentially a bus stop – yes, that's correct.'
'Well if that's so I ask once again – who by?'
'By the creature that waits there.'
'And that's the reason you won't pass by it on your own?'
'Exactly. He might see me and make me wait with him again.'
'But if you're with other people that can't happen?'
'I'm not sure, but it seems a lot less likely.'
'Explain this to me.'
'What's to tell? I've told you it all.'
'It's not much of a tale for an event of forty years' duration.'

Springer paused and sighed:
'Time itself means very little; what is there to say of an accountant's life even if he lives to be a hundred? Nothing very much happened to me in those forty years so there's nothing much to recount.'

'Go on, Bob,' said Disvan. 'You ought to tell him the full story.'

Springer took this in, and then turned to address me:
'Do you want that? Do you genuinely want to understand why I am as I am?'

'Yes,' I replied in all truthfulness, 'tell me how you were

deprived of the days of your youth.'

'My youth? Yes, that's what I lost I suppose and my young manhood and early middle age as well. I was only in my twenties when I was captured you see.'

'How did it occur?'

'On an ordinary day – or evening to be more precise. I was going to get a bus from Binscombe into Guildford to see a movie; on my own as usual. It was about sevenish. I was done up to the nines and I can remember very clearly that the sun was almost down and it was drizzling. The shelter wasn't there in those days – just the stop and the bench set back from the road and I recall getting quite wet and feeling miserable.'

'Then, just a few moments before the bus would arrive (for you could trust the timetables then) I heard a voice call me by name. That surprised me because I'd thought I was alone, but when I turned round I could see that there was an old man sitting on the seat and he was beckoning me. There didn't seem to be anything really amiss although I felt sure there'd been no one on the seat when I'd arrived. Even so, I put that out of my mind for I very often travelled from that stop and consequently felt pretty much at ease there.

'How can I help you?' I said, going up close to the person who'd spoken to me. It was nearly dark by that time you see and all I could make out was the outline of the old boy.

'*You can wait with me,*' he said back.

'Well, I didn't like his tone at all; it sounded very bitter, vicious almost, but I was an obliging sort of young man, very reluctant to give offence (more fool me) and so I said, 'Very well' and sat down beside him.

'Do I know you?' I enquired, for he'd approached me by name.

'*No,*' he said, '*but I know you.*'

'How so?'

'*Because I've often seen you here.*'

Well, he sounded so nasty and unfriendly that I let it go at that and we waited on in silence.'

'Till when?'

'Till the bus arrived, Mr Oakley. Then by the light the bus gave out I saw that it was no man I was sitting alongside, leastways it may have been a man once but no longer.

Horrible it was, pink and shrivelled and hairless and the skin on its face was taut and shiny. I could see its bared teeth and empty eye-sockets and it said:

'*You can wait with me.*'

As you might imagine, I screamed and went to make a run for it but found I couldn't. No noise came from my lips and I remained rooted to my seat next to that ... thing.'

'What about the bus?'

'That was almost the worst bit. The buses always stopped, you see, just to check there was no one waiting on the bench since that was usually in shadow. I stared straight at the driver and, as I thought, he looked straight back at me.

'I even, in my distress, waved my arms at him but then he just turned his head and drove off. I realized then that, the Lord have mercy on me, I was no longer visible to the world of men.

'I watched, with a yearning I can't convey to you, the lights of the bus go off into the distance and the thing beside me chuckled — the sort of laugh cruel children make and that's when it all began.'

'For forty solid years?'

'Almost, but not quite to the day. Buses came and went (with decreasing frequency as the years went by, I might add) queues formed and then boarded, day succeeded day and season succeeded season but still I was held there.'

'But what about food and drink, what about winter weather, cramp and things of that nature?'

'I never seemed to be hungry or thirsty, the cold and wind passed around me and whatever happened in the real world appeared not to be applicable to me. All I was allowed to do was wait: wait with that foul creature.'

'That's appalling!'

'You can't imagine how appalling. Please don't get the impression that I didn't try to save myself because for the first few weeks I did little else. Every bus that arrived I begged and pleaded to be allowed to board it and every queue that formed I shouted and waved at but, all in all, I might just as well have saved my breath. People I'd grown up with waited just a few feet away, some even sat on the seat with us but none of them could see or hear me.

'Once, my dear mother, God rest her soul, came there and waited for a bus and I nearly went berserk trying to catch her attention. She seemed to realize something was wrong for she got fidgety and uneasy and kept looking round for what it was that was disturbing her but when she did she looked straight through me.

'Eventually her bus came and she got on and once she was sitting down she stared at the bench as if she knew her son was sitting there and she continued to look as the bus drew away. That was very bitter ...

'I never saw her again for I later found out that she died soon after.

'How that creature laughed to see my tears that day and his every laugh sounded like the death of a baby on Christmas Eve. In my fury and horror I struck him but his flesh burned like acid and where I'd touched him my skin smoked – look, the scars still show.'

It was true, a wide band of skin across each of his knuckles was brownish, twisted and quite dead.

'After that experience it was hard to imagine anything worse happening and so, after a fashion, I resigned myself to my fate. Still I asked to board each bus that came but the creature would just snap "*No!*" in its nasty voice and that was that.

'With the passing of the years I grew to be almost philosophical about my predicament and took pleasure in watching the leaves on the trees change colour and all the other slow annual mutations in the rest of nature – that was something I'd never had the time for up to then. Bit by bit I observed different buses come into service, all efficient and new, and then see them pass through their working lives till their engines were crotchety and their livery battleworn. Watching the changes in people's fashions was interesting too, spring clothes, winter clothes and then back to spring again and new styles kept appearing as well – quite fascinating really, if you've got nothing else to do.

'There were also moments of relative excitement like when workmen came to erect a shelter and light in ... 1973 I think and when an advertising hoarding was put up about a year later. After that I had the pleasure of watching the advertisement posters being changed at regular intervals and it allowed me to keep in touch with things in some small way.

'I noticed that I was getting older but since otherwise time was suspended for me I learnt just to relax and observe which is something few other people have the opportunity to do in this world. In time, you see, all of life passed by my bus stop.'

'You make it sound almost idyllic!'

'No it wasn't that for I was held against my will, remember, and that fact coloured everything else. And, if the creature even suspected that I was taking pleasure in something, it would talk to me.'

'What about?'

'It's best, believe me, for your sake that you do not know. Suffice it to say that he said bitter and twisted things – of individuals queuing for a bus for instance – that showed people in a low and degraded light or emphasized the misery and futility of human life as he saw it. Of course his words were designed to produce an effect in me – whether they also represented the truth or not I've no idea.'

'How did it end?'

'As simply as it began. One day a bus arrived as per normal and the creature said, "*Here is your bus.*" Suddenly I found that I could move and I saw that the driver's eyes were focused on me – he could actually see me! Despite forty years' disuse my legs could still carry as if I'd merely had a short sit-down and, as you might expect, I was on that bus like a streak of lightning. Then, just as the doors closed behind me, I heard the creature say, "*Thank you for waiting with me.*" The doors slid shut and when I turned round to look I couldn't see the thing even though the last words it'd said were still ringing in my ears. Then the bus pulled away and took me back to Binscombe.

'That wasn't the end of all my problems by any means; in effect one major affliction was replaced with myriad minor ones for you can't just leave your life for forty years and expect to take up the reins again on your return. Difficulties began from the moment I boarded that long delayed bus: take for instance the problem with paying my fare. I'd missed out on decimal currency you see, I knew nothing about it and the driver wouldn't accept the coins I offered him; he thought I was either drunk or a joker offering him three old pennies. When he told me how much the fare really was it was my turn to think that it was he who was joking – inflation being another thing I'd yet to learn about.

'Anyway, to cut a long story short, my mother's house had been sold many years before, I'd paid no National Insurance so there was no pension awaiting me, most of my old friends were dead or gone away and all in all I had to start from scratch.

'In time, of course, everything came together; I found a place to live, I caught up on forty years of world history in the public library, I even got married, though God knows why (begging your pardon, Disvan) and here I am. My life's not so bad but I've got a lot of catching up to do and that's why I've no intention of ever being made to wait for a bus again.'

'Do you think then that the creature is still there?'

'I'm not sure, I just assume it is and act accordingly. You see, I've been free for a number of years now and for all I know the thing may be getting lonely and in need of company again so I'm not inclined to put the matter to the test.'

'And that's why you won't pass the bus stop on your own.'

'Exactly.' He paused, something clearly bothering him, and then continued in a rush of words: 'Tell me, Mr Oakley, do you believe that what I've told you is true?'

I considered the possibility of this while studying Springer's guileless, indeed vacant, face and found that a honest answer came to me easily.

'I've only lived in this place a short time but long enough not to totally discount what you say.'

'That is a good answer – if slightly enigmatic,' said Disvan.

'Mr Disvan believes me, don't you?'

'I do Bob, I accept what you tell us but what I don't accept, as I've said to you many times before, is that you're in any further danger. You've done your stint of waiting and your company is no longer required.'

'Fine words but I'll not believe them till I'm safely in my grave.'

'As you wish.'

I felt some need to make amends for my earlier incivility and in debt to Springer for his candidness.

'In that case,' I said, 'I – or perhaps we ...' Disvan nodded in affirmation, 'would be happy on this occasion to provide an escort to your house.'

The old man nodded his thanks.

'I'll not impose on your good nature with any regularity but tonight I would welcome a short walk home and human company on the way. I'm obliged to you. After all,' he said wistfully, 'at my late stage of life I just haven't got the time to wait for a bus.'

VII

The Band in the Park

Jean Stubbs

To return to the place of one's childhood after forty years' absence, after forty years' varied exile, is to encounter the final exile of all. For nothing is the same.

Throughout her marriage, as Jack followed his job from one city to another, from one country to another, Kate nourished secret strength in old roots. When he retires, she used to think, we'll take a house there. Not a big house, but big enough for the grandchildren to stay, big enough to hold a family Christmas party. Then everything will come full circle and we can settle down at last. Everything will join neatly together and make a new whole, with ourselves at the centre.

Then he died very suddenly, in a few minutes on a Sunday evening, and took her centre with him. So that she behaved distractedly and sought to evade grief by action, and severed the roots she had by finding just the house they would have looked for. The excitement of moving, of organising a different regime, appeased her temporarily. She wrote many letters, highlighting the few facets of a blossoming friendship, an evening class on painting at the Institute, the discovery of her mother's former charwoman – still hale, and willing to help out. She was amusing over shortcomings: the buses that stopped running at 10.30 p.m., the fierce in-fighting for power on small local committees. She wrote to convince herself rather than her family, and perhaps her desperation seeped through because they sent Polly to stay with her for a month.

Uplifted, Kate turned one of her spare rooms into a nursery, and papered her way through the first anniversary of Jack's death. She weltered in plans for afternoon walks, individual rice puddings, stories read by the fire before bedtime. She returned for the moment, in her first grandchild, to the humble pleasures of her own children. She was able again to create, in her vacuum, the feeling of security she had generated for them – in spite of frequent changes and wanderings. She became again the still centre of their existence: the one who made home, though the packing cases were standing in strange rooms: the one who knew where this toy, that book, could be located among a jungle of straw and paper: the one who turned a scratch meal into a special picnic. She was wanted again.

But Polly said, after the flurry of arrival was over. 'Who shall I play with?' and this Kate had forgotten.

The charwoman's great-grandchildren, somewhat older and considerably tougher than Polly, were brought on to the scene with small success. They were first awed by the bountiful tea, the bountiful toys from two generations. Then they found the doll's house and the meccano sets were poor exchange for spacemen and guns. They preferred the television to a story. In the end they huddled together and whispered and giggled, while Polly stood self-consciously apart. Damaged for her, Kate gave them sweets and sent them home as soon as she decently could.

'Did you play with children like that when you were a little girl?' Polly asked, politely astonished.

Remembering a similar isolation, accentuated by the social barriers of the late 1920s, Kate said, 'I was often alone.' She had forgotten that, too.

'Wasn't it very nice when you were a little girl?'

'Oh yes!' said Kate loyally, emphatically. 'We had lots of things to do. Why, we used to have a band in the park. Here, let me show you.'

She held Polly up to the sitting-room window, but the park had also changed. Autumn stripped the trees and denuded the floral clock. A cold wind wrinkled the waters of the ornamental lake. The grass was no longer so green and lush, the walks no longer as spacious. On the rising knoll, which had once seemed an emerald hill crowned in splendour, stood the skeleton of an iron bandstand.

'Of course, it's old and rusty and empty now,' said Kate

apologetically. 'And, anyway, they're going to make a children's playground in that area, so they'll be pulling it down. The next time you come,' she offered, 'there'll be swings and a paddling pool, and all sorts of jolly things.'

Polly contemplated the bandstand.

'Was it pretty?'

'Very pretty. Bright green, with scarlet lines down the posts, and gold twiddly bits on the corners. The bandmaster was called Enoch Higginbottom, and he wore a beautiful uniform with gold braid on the shoulders.'

And the brass instruments glistened, the music sheets were laundry-white in delicate black stands.

'Did they *live* in that umbrella house?'

'Oh no, they had their own homes. But they played for us in the park on Sundays, when the weather was fine.'

Rain streamed down the window, blurring the vision on the knoll.

'Where is the band now?'

'Dead and gone,' said Kate.

'I'm not going to die. Not ever,' said Polly.

She breathed on the pane and polished it clean with her handkerchief.

'That's better,' she observed. 'When the rain stops can we have a walk in the park and feed the ducks?'

*

'What did the band play?' Polly asked, as a flotilla of ducks set sail for the bobbing bread, and were routed by the swan.

'I don't think you'd know any of the tunes my love. Waltzes, like *The Blue Danube*. Marches, like *Pomp and Circumstance*. Songs like *Ye Banks and Braes*. All sorts of tunes.'

'How long ago was it when you were a little girl like me? Is it about a hundred years since the band played?'

Kate decoyed the swan with a crust, and they watched his majestic greed.

'It's about forty-five years since I was a little girl like you, and the last time I heard the band was the summer before the war. Thirty ... six ... years ago,' said Kate, covering a smile.

Polly, who was never going to die, found this an eternity.

'Goodness me!' she said, in brisk imitation of her mother's

voice. 'What a very long time. Shall we go home now, by the bandstand? Can I climb up into the band's little house? By myself?'

'Yes, I should think so. It's quite safe, if dilapidated. But stand in the middle, don't go near the rails, and walk carefully up the steps.'

Polly's skipping-rope smacked purposefully along the paths. Reaching her objective she stopped, wound the cord round the coloured handles, and handed it to her grandmother.

'So's I shan't trip over it,' she explained. '*What* was the bandsman's name?'

'Bandmaster. Enoch Higginbottom.'

Polly stood on the first step and lifted her head. From Kate's house across the park this bandstand had seemed toy-size. Now it reared above the child, a peeling iron temple. The wind blew hollow music under the roof. Leaves scurried across the floor.

'May I come up, Mr Higginbottom?' called Polly.

She listened to the sound of wind and leaves enraptured.

'Mr Higginbottom says yes I can.'

She paused on the top step, shook hands with an imaginary bandmaster, and stood by his side, soldier-straight.

'They're playing a special tune for me,' she informed Kate. Her woollen scarf flipped rebellious tassels over both shoulders. 'Can you guess what it is?'

'*Hickory, Dickory, Dock.*'

'No! They're playing *Polly Put the Kettle on. We'll all have tea.*'

'A very good idea.' said Kate shivering in the November sun.

'That's my gran'ma, Mr Higginbottom,' said Polly ignoring her hint. 'When she was a little girl a long long time ago, she used to listen to your band. She's very pleased to see you again. Who played the ter-ter-ter, gran'ma?'

'Jackie Cleethorpe was the best trumpeter.'

'Is he big and fat with a red face?'

'No, that was Ernest Proctor. Jackie was small and thin and pale.'

'Did their faces come out like this, when they blew?'

And Polly's bright cheeks distended dreadfully.

'Yes, and we used to watch – in case they burst like balloons.'

'Well, that's all for now,' said Polly firmly, shaking hands with the invisible Enoch Higginbottom. 'Thank you very much. We'll come again tomorrow.'

She hopped down the fretted steps tongue between teeth, and took Kate's hand.

'You see, they don't have to be dead and gone if you just make your mind up,' she said severely, and turned and waved from the iron gates. 'Oh, look, it's all new again!'

And in the last of the sunlight, with rain to lend a spurious shine, the bandstand did indeed seem rejuvenated.

'Do they have their tea there, or do they go home?'

'They used to go home for tea.'

Polly ran back to the park gates and shouted. 'You can go home to tea now, band!' And waited. 'They're just packing up their ter-ter-ters. They won't be a minute.' Then she pushed the gate as wide as it would go, short legs toiling, stood aside and saluted. 'Good afternoon, band,' she said, to the departing musicians. And closed it carefully after them.

*

'Was you a good girl for grandma?' asked Mrs Bowker, comforting her knees in front of the kitchen range.

'Now and then,' said Polly truthfully.

Child of a new age, she surveyed this relic of an old era with polite fascination.

'You should be a good girl all the while, not now and again.'

'Oh, I couldn't be good *all* the time,' said Polly honestly.

'*My* great-grandchilder is. I see to that.'

'Ted isn't,' said Polly. 'He threw a stone at gran'ma's cat.'

'Let me take your coat and hat,' said Kate diplomatically. 'You can wash your hands at the sink, unless you want to go upstairs.'

'You didn't ought to let her answer back like that,' said Mrs Bowker, brushing aside the diplomacy. 'I wouldn't put up with it from any of mine, I can tell you.'

'We were looking at the old bandstand,' said Kate, unable to reconcile a gap of three generations and a different set of values.

'Smack her bottom, I would, if she was mine.'

'Did you know Mr Higginbottom?' asked Polly, connecting the word with the name.

'Owd Enoch?' Happily sidetracked. 'Eh, I did that. He were related on my mam's side of the family. He allus carried a paper of humbugs in his pocket to give to the childer. Why, he gave *me* sweets when I were a little lass.'

Seeing Polly about to frame some unforgivable question, Kate said, 'Hush! Don't you want to listen?'

'I've scrubbed the kitchen floor,' said Mrs Bowker in a monotone, thinking of something else, 'and peeled a pan of potatoes, missis. And done the ironing, and blacked the range ...'

The recital was automatic, given every Friday afternoon. When she had worked for Kate's mother, as a young woman. Kate remembered the same words delivered in the same tone. They had come full circle, and arrived back at the place they started from. So Kate brewed the tea as her mother had done, and Polly watched Mrs Bowker suck it thoughtfully into her mouth as Kate had done, and all was peace and hot buttered toast.

'Eh! Enoch Higginbottom,' said Mrs Bowker, staring into the furnace of coke, entranced. 'Why, he passed on during the last war. He were a fire warden or summat. Though he must have been going on seventy, by then. Dropped dead in't street. It were his heart, not the bombs, as did it.'

'And did you know Jackie Cleethorpe? Please?' said Polly, eating and watching.

'Aye, I did that. He were drowned at Dunkirk, poor lad. His folk was Cleethorpe's Butchers, but he allus looked as if he could do with a square meal.'

'What's a square meal, please?'

Kate had a simultaneous vision of a square plate full of squared food, and said, 'Not what you think, Polly.'

'And there were Billy Thwaites, as blew the trombone. He died in't desert. Eh, I wouldn't like to die that far from home, under't blazing sun ...'

One by one, with the memory of the very old for what is past, she peopled the bandstand.

'Jimmy Dewhurst, now. He couldn't say a word for

stutting. His dad tried to belt him out of it, but he stutted worse nor ever, then. But give him a drum to thump and he knew what was what. Aye, and poor Tom Nuttall, as they never had a good word for – till he died for king and country. They fetched him home to be buried, and there were that many wreaths. His mam said folk should give flowers to the living, not wreaths to the dead. That's what she said. All local lads. Our brass band. Best in all England …'

They sat twenty strong, in their dark blue uniforms tricked out with white sashes, with brass buttons and gold braid, waiting for all the fall of the baton. The summer of 1939 was long and hot and beautiful: a finale to the age that was passing.

'So they all died in the war, one way or another?' said Kate. 'I hadn't realised. We were evacuated, of course. And then, I've been away more or less ever since.'

'Aye, young and middling and owd. They all died. Every one. After the war things changed. We never had another band like that one, and now we never shall.'

'Why not, please?' asked Polly, stringing honey from jar to spoon.

'Don't talk with your mouth full,' said Mrs Bowker. 'Why not? Because they're pulling the bandstand down to make way for the playground. That's why not. And folk never listen in the park, of a Sunday – and Sunday ain't what it were, neither. If folk want a bit of music they turns their wireless on. And it ain't the same.' She woke up to the present. 'And what's got into you, Polly? You never bothered wi't bandstand afore today.'

'I was too young to understand it when I arrived,' said Polly seriously.

Mrs Bowker chuckled.

'Too young? You were born owd, my lass. Owd-fashioned!' She ruminated. 'Well, I'll be off, missis. I've scrubbed the kitchen floor, and peeled a pan of potatoes, as well as the ironing, and blacked the range …'

She placed the money carefully in three separate compartments of a rubbed purse, and snapped it shut. Pulled her shawl from the back of the door and swathed her head and shoulders. Wrapped both hands and purse in the plaid folds.

'You be a good girl for grandma,' she cautioned, as she lifted the latch and stepped out into the early evening.

Polly lifted her eyebrows significantly, and shrugged.

'Sometimes Mrs Bowker gets me down,' she observed. 'And all that about her great-grandchildren. Ted is a very rude boy. If I was a rude girl I'd tell you what he said to me. But I'm not. And I didn't. Can I have a piece of cake now? I've eaten all my toast.'

Kate sliced the sponge-cake and said, 'You needn't play with him.'

'How old is Mrs Bowker, if I may ask?'

'Old enough to be my mother.'

'Then why does she do your work for you?'

'Because she needs to work and she needs the money.'

'If she's very old she should have more money, shouldn't she?'

Kate could find no adequate reply, except, 'Yes, but unfortunately she hasn't.'

'Once she was a little girl, and listened to the band,' said Polly.

*

Rain or fine, each afternoon they walked in the park, and watched the workmen marking out the new playground.

'But why don't they leave the bandstand for the children to play in?' asked Polly.

'They can play better on the swings and roundabouts.'

'But they could listen to the band instead, and have their very own tunes. That's nicer.'

'I'm afraid all children haven't got your imagination,' said Kate. 'And they might fall through the rails or hurt themselves on the steps.'

'But why can't they put the playground further away, and have the bandstand as well?'

'Because that would mean spoiling the floral clock.'

'But the floral clock doesn't play your very own tunes.'

'Old people like Mrs Bowker prefer to sit on the benches and look at the floral clock in the summer. Now you feed the ducks, and I'll feed the swan. I wonder what Mr Higginbottom will play for you today?'

Polly's orange tights were stout with importance.

'I'll bet it's *Jingle Bells*, even though it isn't Christmas yet!'

'I'll bet you're right,' said Kate.

The band, fleshed by Mrs Bowker, flowering in the hothouse of Polly's fancy, developed a ghostly reality. They lost their first angelic perfection and became human enough to err, as they had erred in life.

'Mr Higginbottom is making them begin All Over Again!' Polly announced, and clapped her woollen hands to her mouth in delight. 'Mr Cleethorpe made two mistakes that time. And Mr Dewhurst stutted when he should have been thumping his drum.'

'I hope they get it right soon,' Kate warned, 'because the park keeper shuts the gates at five o'clock this Friday.'

'Oh, they will, gran'ma. Truly. Just little mistakes. Excuse me, but we have to hush now because Mr Higginbottom is starting them with his stick.'

*

Once again Kate encountered the infinite delicacy and cunning of a child's mind. Her own memories were too sketchy for Polly's information. Polly needed hard facts to support her imagination, and as many of them as possible. The obvious source was Mrs Bowker, and on her ancient altar Polly sacrificed small truths and sharp observations.

'Was you a good girl for grandma today?'

'Yes, Mrs Bowker.'

'That's right, then. My great-grandchilder is allus good.'

'Yes, Mrs Bowker.'

'You carry on like them and you won't go far wrong.'

'No, Mrs Bowker.'

'That's a good girl, then.'

Polly waited, red-cheeked, robin-eyed, while the old woman dozed over her tea and warmed her knees. Closer and a little closer, until the round face hovered by the wrinkled one.

'Please tell me about the band.'

'Eh! Forever worriting about that band! Well, it were a right good 'un. The best in all England.'

'Did the Queen ever listen to it?'

'The Queen? Why, she were nobbut a little lass like your

grandma, afore the war.'

'But didn't she come here just the same?'

'Never as I know on. But the old King and Queen, her grandad and grandma, King George and Queen Mary that was – *they* come to the Town *H*all in Jubilee Year,' and in their honour Mrs Bowker aspirated the *H* most dreadfully. 'They stood on't balcony with the Lord Mayor. Eh! he were as ignorant as pigs in Dublin, that chap. I felt ashamed. Still, they was very genteel with him. Smiling and waving and that.'

'They must have heard the band, mustn't they?'

Mrs Bowker pondered. She stirred. She nodded.

'Aye, now you mention it. They played *God Save the King*.'

'In the bandstand, with flags, and the King and Queen in their golden crowns.'

'Nay, you daft lass! In front o't Town *H*all.'

Polly regretted this, but other diversions beckoned.

'Tell me about Alfie Moss, when the wasp buzzed round his head and he had to keep on blowing.'

'I were on't front row, and I could see the sweat on his face from where I was sat! Eh! Laugh!' She laughed again in recollection, then sobered. 'But that lad never stopped blowing,' she accused Polly. 'Don't say a word agin him. He never stopped blowing.'

'He was a very brave lad,' said Polly gravely. 'Tell me about …'

The band played again: pride of the town. Pompous grave, of an indifferent talent and unmindful of discrepancies. There was the time when Jimmy Dewhurst, obscured by the magnificence of his drum, failed to see where the band was going and took the wrong turning.

'Though he should've known by that time,' said Mrs Bowker, 'as they allus went down Ellis Street, never up Windy Brew. There he were, thumping along, all by hisself.'

There was the time when the music sheets were unaccountably disarranged, and half the band played *The Merry Widow Waltz*, and the other half pursued *The Bluebells of Scotland*.'

'But owd Enoch kept them at it, till they finished up together.'

There was the time when Enoch started them at too quick a

tempo, and some were lost on the way. Though all played manfully, if red and puzzled by this turn of events.

'Anyway, they was good at stopping,' said Mrs Bowker. 'Whenever he come down with his stick they stopped, whether they'd finished or not. That's the way you tell a good band from a bad 'un.'

'But once Jackie Cleethorpe played all by himself, didn't he?'

'Aye, he did that. Tootle, tootle, all by hisself. He were musical, you see. He were listening to hisself, until owd Enoch shouted at him.'

'What did he shout, Mrs Bowker?'

'He shouted, "Shurrup, will you, Jackie?" '

Mrs Bowker slapped her knees and laughed.

'Tell me about ...' would spark further revelations to life.

'Oh, I remember ...' Kate might say, and another forgotten door swung open. Of no importance, really, but holding warmth and value.

*

Children shut out what they cannot bear to acknowledge. Polly had seen the playground's skeleton emerge, had known the bandstand must go, and ignored these facts.

'When is she off home, missis?' asked the charwoman.

'Next Saturday.'

'Well, that's a good thing,' said Mrs Bowker, with surprising perception. 'The council'll never shift off their fat backsides fast enough to start pulling owt down afore she goes.'

'I hope not.'

'And she'll have plenty to think on, when she gets back. And then, the next time she comes she'll have forgot all about it.'

Mrs Bowker peeled the potatoes so lavishly that Kate wondered how she had ever survived the Depression. But perhaps old age rendered her careless, or Kate's potatoes could afford to lose more flesh than those of poor folk.

'Because she's fanciful, missis,' pursued the charwoman. 'Our Ruby were fanciful – the one as died young.'

To be fanciful was not synonymous with survival.

'I remember Ruby. She was a pretty little girl.'

'Aye, and your mam used to let her play with you and your brother. Which were more nor I can say about t'others I worked for! Snotty-nosed set of nowts! Our Ruby were as good as them, and better. I'm rough, missis, allus was and allus will be. But our Ruby were a lady.'

She wiped her eyes on her sleeve, and attacked the potatoes.

'Any road,' she remarked more cheerfully, 'them fat fools'll never stir off their backsides.'

But they did.

Kate was wakened at eight o'clock the following Friday by Polly running into her room crying. 'Don't let them! Don't let them!'

The opening chords of destruction punctuated her appeal.

'But you knew, my little love, you knew it would happen,' said Kate, helpless.

'How could I ever believe it?' She clung round Kate's neck. 'I know,' she cried, lifting a wet and suddenly radiant face, 'you just go out there, gran'ma, and tell them in your special voice to Stop It At Once.'

'I'm afraid they wouldn't listen.'

'They have to!' said Polly, with absolute faith.

'Polly, no one can stop them. It's all been arranged for such a long time.'

'Not the *mayor* can't stop them? Not the *Queen*?'

'Not anyone,' said Kate.

She saw faith falter and vanish, and was devastated.

'Then what's the use of you all?' Polly demanded, of a world of powerless adults.

She pushed Kate away, and scrambled off the bed. Beating on the window of her bedroom she shouted. 'What about Mr Higginbottom and his band, you bad things? Where will Mr Higginbottom and the band play now? Don't you care? Don't you care?'

The iron crescendos crushed her. She crawled under the bedclothes and pulled them over her head.

'In a right taking, is she?' asked Mrs Bowker, removing her shawl. 'I said she would be. I said. That's what comes of being fanciful. Our Ruby were fanciful. Happen you recollect her? The one as died young.'

All day they felled and carted. All day Polly stayed beneath the bedclothes and refused food and comfort. In the evening there was silence, and a space where the bandstand had once been. Kate found the child standing in her nightgown, staring into the dusk, resigned.

'Would you like to speak to Mummy on the telephone?' Kate asked.

The small back rejected her advances. One shoulder hunched a protest.

'Or would you like to speak to Daddy instead? He'll be coming tomorrow afternoon to collect you in the car.'

'Could *he* have stopped them?' Polly demanded, over her hunched shoulder.

'No, he couldn't.'

'Then what's the use?' But her accusation now lacked sting.

'Oh, pop your dressing-gown on and come downstairs,' said Kate. 'I'm baking a potato in its jacket for your supper. And I've made a rice pudding in the blue-striped dish, just for you.'

'Has Mrs Bowker gone home?'

'Yes, and she said good-bye to you, and left you a ten-penny piece, and said see you in the spring.'

'She shouldn't have done that!' Polly said crossly. 'Now she's made me sorry for being fed up with her.'

Kate sat on the bed, and laughed until Polly joined in.

'Come on, get dressed, and you can stay up late for once. You've been sulking in bed all day.'

'Sulking? Sulking?' Polly cried, pulling her nightgown over her head. 'I've been *sorrowing*! Can't you tell the difference?'

By the parlour fire, replete, she rearranged the contents of the doll's house while Kate read aloud.

'I had imaginary playmates when I was your age,' said Kate, setting down *The Hobbit*, taking off her reading glasses.

'Were they real?'

'In one way. Not real like real people.'

'Could you see them?'

'Not exactly. But I knew what they looked like.'

'That's not as nice as seeing them.'

Kate surveyed her grand-daughter with interest, and dared ask the question.

'Could you see the band?'

'Yes,' said Polly. 'Couldn't you?'
'Not with my eyes, but with my mind.'
'Couldn't you hear them?'
'Only in my head, remembering.'
'Dear me,' said Polly in her mother's voice. Then, to salve any possible wound. 'Never mind, you can see the Cat.'

That ghostly inhabitant of the house, whose presence confounded the real cat, and occasionally confused Kate. No fearful visitation, this feline spirit of some one else's past. A shape on the stairs, a walking shadow in the rooms. Even Mrs Bowker had been known to address it and then blame the mistake on her failing eyesight.

'Oh yes, I see him.' Kate admitted.

'Then perhaps one day you'll see the band,' said Polly. 'Isn't it about time I went to bed? We don't want Mummy asking if I was up at all hours, do we?'

On their way upstairs in companionable mood, Kate ventured further.

'If you can see the band, then you should be able to see the bandstand, surely. As it was, too.'

'I expect so.'

'Which was far prettier and brighter. So why all the drama about a rusty old heap of iron being knocked down?'

Polly's chin lifted. That desecration would not be forgiven.

'Because they hurt its feelings,' she declared. 'Clanging it about!'

'But it doesn't really matter in the end, does it?'

Polly considered.

'It matters like that rude Ted Bowker throwing a stone at your cat.'

'Oh, I see. It matters in that way, if not in the other.'

'Just so,' said Polly gravely.

*

The house was empty without her. Old toys and special crockery went back into their cupboards. The nursery became simply a spare room.

The hive of one's inner world grows no smaller with

increasing age, but none of the cells is filled all of the time. Nevertheless there was much to do. Friendships to be kept in good repair. The house to be made welcome. The garden to grow. The several creations of hands and mind. Mrs Bowker to be made to feel indispensable, though nowadays corners harboured fluff and washed surfaces needed a final rinse. But Kate regretted the sense of wonder which had left with Polly. Adults know too much, and too little.

They do not see the band in its glory. They know that deprivation lies behind the proudly distended cheeks, that working clothes supplant the splendid uniforms. They know that the band must die.

This is going to be a bad night, thought Kate, and accepted its onslaught. The past was all mourning and defeat. Everyone set out, like Polly, with a great wonder and belief, and endured the whittling which would end in oblivion. Life was a tragedy, a series of battles to be won or lost, which would anyway end in final defeat. The only choice lay in the way you approached the terror: with gallantry, stoicism or a shriek of despair. A bad night.

She walked the house, and Enoch Higginbottom's weak heart leaped for the last time. A boy drowned at Dunkirk within sight of his rescuers, because he had never learned to swim. Another shrivelled beneath a pitiless sun. Those who had never sent flowers to the living now honoured the dead with many wreaths. She knew the life-in-death of heart and body. She shrank before the accumulating sorrows of the world, and a legion of ghosts marched upon her, demanding succour or explanation. She could neither answer nor save them.

In Polly's room she looked sombrely through the moonlit window, to embrace a vacancy which would not be ignored.

And there on the knoll stood a child's paradise. The freshly painted bandstand rivalled the emerald grass. The knobs were celestial gold, the scarlet lines life-blood. From every point of the canopy, pennants flew. Beneath it, resplendent in their uniforms, sat the members of the band. Their music sheets were tablets of ivory sprinkled with ebony notes. The brilliance of their instruments most pleasantly hurt the eyes.

Before them, twirling black moustaches (everyone swore he dyed them), swelled Enoch Higginbottom in his prime. His baton was both earthly and celestial sceptre, the ultimate symbol of power. All the chairs were out, and filled with listeners and spectators. In the front row on two gold thrones, sat King George and Queen Mary in Coronation robes.

Momentarily, Kate realised that Polly had improved on the original. Then she relinquished herself to the occasion.

They were playing *God Save the King* and never had she heard them blast it out with such pomp and royalty, with so few mistakes. There was the fat mayor, in full regalia and chain of office. There the mayoress in her best black silk, tightly corseted. A wasp threatened Alfie Moss's dignity, but he blew heroically on. The children sucked ice-cream cornets. The adults sat grand and uncomfortable in their Sunday clothes. They had surmounted the ills of the world and proclaimed the moment.

The applause of thousands greeted the final bars, and the band took a bow – eyes fixed reverently on the King and Queen. Then the clapping became frantic because Enoch Higginbottom was introducing a guest conductor.

Polly had evidently thought out her appearance with some care. She wore her white nylon party dress. A tangerine satin bow bound her long black hair. Her slippers were mirrors of shine, her socks snows of purity. She had borrowed Kate's childhood necklace, and a fine gold bracelet embraced her left arm. Kate could not place the bracelet anywhere in time past or present.

Polly curtsied deeply to the visiting royalty, mounted the rostrum, waited for complete silence. The band poised themselves for a moment on her uplifted baton, and then swung into a hearty rendering of *Polly Put the Kettle on*.

The scene faded back into the knoll, but left no sadness behind it. Restored, Kate went downstairs and set her own kettle on the range.

I must give Polly that necklace now, instead of later, she thought. But where did the bracelet come from? She must have wanted a gold bracelet. I could buy it for her birthday. And I shall write her a long letter tomorrow and tell her I saw the band. I could paint a picture of it, too. She'd like that. She'd hang it up in her bedroom.

So what is time, and what is reality? Out in the park, which is empty now, the shadows hold secrets and the moon shines. But for those who can see and hear, the band still plays.

VIII

The Indian's Grave

Ross McKay

'That's it right there. Can't you see it?' I remember straining my young eyes, following my great-uncle's gnarled brown finger with the tobacco-stained nail as it pointed towards an area of greener corn midway across the verdant field.

'Yeah ... yes, I can, Uncle Joe.' And I could too. There really was a patch that was darker than the area around it. At first I'd thought it was wishful thinking but the longer I stared the more I became convinced that what I saw had not merely been suggested by old Joe's insistent tone.

'Course ya can, boy. It's there all right. Just like my Daddy showed me when I was 'bout your years. And *he* knew for sure, cause it was *his* Daddy that shot the pore critter.'

He wheezed with old man's laughter, eyes crinkling as he looked to me to join in.

'But why, why did he shoot him, Uncle Joe?'

'What's that gun for, Johnny?' The .22 cradled in my plaid-shirted arm had not been fired that day, because we'd seen no groundhogs. Perplexed by such an obvious question, I pondered the familiar weather-beaten face framed in the inevitable battered felt hat, thinking before I answered simply, 'To shoot pests, like Grandma said.'

My late Grandmother had always maintained that guns should be kept for that purpose alone, unless to kill for food. 'Well, Edna was right ... mostly,' allowed her brother, who missed her as much as I did. 'In my grandfolk's day, the Indians were pests. Worse than! Land's sakes Johnny, ain't your school-teachers ever taught you 'bout the Ojibway and the Hurons? They were downright murderous.'

The teachers had never dwelt on the subject of the Indians who had trodden these hills and woods long before our ancestors had left the over-farmed lands of Ulster. Like most of Ontario's teachers in the early Fifties, they taught history in terms of the origins of the people whose taxes paid their salaries, Scotland, England, Northern Ireland, Wales, all got a mention in class; the French, whom nobody cared for very much, were covered in the lesson that dealt with General Wolfe and the Heights of Abraham. Then the children would sing of how the 'Thistle, Shamrock, Rose Entwine, the Maple Leaf Forever.'

So my knowledge of the red men was limited to what I gleaned from comics or from the movies. We had two such theatres in town, the Avon and the Vogue, which regularly featured massacres and ambushes whereby the Sioux and the Apaches invariably came off the worse. At 13, however, I had enough savvy to realise that there was more to it than that. But as the son of a hard-headed farmer, I seldom had the opportunity or encouragement to read up on Indian lore. So I relished Uncle Joe's tales of yore.

'Course they maybe had a right to be. Murderous, you see? This here land was their huntin' ground – full of deer, and fish in the rivers, then. Poor fellows – all we left them was their *happy hunting grounds.*'

'But *who* was *he*?' I gestured at the mid-field patch of green he had pin-pointed earlier.

'Don't know for sure, Johnny. I heard tell he was the chief, or the last of his tribe, or could'a been both, I guess. He came round one night after our people had settled here and killed a cow. Butchered it right yonder, where I showed you. Seems my Grandpa came out from the cabin – was jest a log affair they lived in then – and found him cuttin' it up. There was some talk I don't rightly recall ...' He frowned, remembering conversations from the nineteenth century, when he had perched alongside the grown-ups at the big maple table. 'Yeah, the old Indian was howlin' and hollerin', like a heathen chant, y'know. Doc Rutherford, he had more books than the library in town today, he claimed the redskin wasn't aimin' to eat it at all. More like a *sacrifice*, he said ...' The old man savoured the unfamiliar word, redolent of Old Testament scriptures.

'So how come he got shot, Uncle Joe?'

It was the first time I had ever seen him embarrassed. Even his tanned face showed a tint of blush.

'Weeeell, ... things weren't so cut and dried in those days. There wasn't so much regard for them as there was for us whites. Grandpa just shot the Indian where he found him. He told us little uns – Lord, I remember him so well, he said, "That savage begged me to shoot him, just raised his war axe and started at me, knew I'd get him before he came within twenty-foot of me." That's what he told us, Johnny. I swallowed it when I was knee high, but I reckon Grandpa just blasted him. Ain't no Indian fool enough to charge rifles ... or was there? I don't know anymore.'

'And he's really buried there?'

The proximity of a real Ojibway, albeit dead for a hundred years and longer, fascinated my youthful fancy more than the moral dilemma which Joe encountered in his long-dead grandfather's narrative.

'Yep, right where he died, war-axe, beads and all. Six feet under, where they laid him the next morning. Grandpa said he wanted it that way and we've ploughed and sowed and harvested over and over again but we've never disturbed the redskin. The old folks said it was his land, his special ground, kinda sacred, y'know.'

I didn't know, not at the age I was then, and maybe if I had, a lot of trouble would've been avoided. Unfortunately, our teacher had been telling us what archaeology was all about, with the pictures of Tutankhamen's tomb, and I figured, reasonably enough, I guess, that what was fitting for an Egyptian pharaoh was good enough for an Ojibway chief. I resolved to dig the Indian up.

That was later in the year, of course. It was a beautiful summer, so it seems, in retrospect. There was Dominion Day to celebrate, then the Orange Walk, when I joined all my male relations and most of our neighbours in the regalia of British loyalism. That was always a high point in my boyhood summers. It seems so long ago, looked at from the cosmopolitan Ontario of the Eighties.

Anyhow it was too fine a summer to be pre-occupied with the dead past. I remember we sang a lot of Hank Williams.

The Indian's Grave

Came the Fall, with everyone out in the fields, I got talking with Larry Dempsey, the kid from the next farm up, while we were watering the horse. As it turned out, it was the horse's last harvest. We were fully mechanised by the following Spring. Larry was in my class and shared my interest in archaeology so we made a pact that when the field was cleared we would excavate the spot Uncle Joe had shown me. We sat on the running boards of the pick-up truck as the grown men crowded around the big tin basin full of home-made lemonade that we'd hauled out from the house, watching them slake their honest thirsts while we speculated on the treasures we might unearth. I particularly coveted the axe-head. Larry was to get the beads.

A week before Thanksgiving, once the field was cropped, Larry and I stole out from our respective homes one moonlit night and, quieting the ever-watchful hounds, made our way up the old dirt road, equipped with spades and flashlights.

The earth was easier to dig than we'd expected, but we'd hardly got started, whispering nervously over our clandestine task, than the moon disappeared behind a large black cloud.

Larry cursed. 'It's creepy, these clouds. Like we're being told to quit digging.' He shivered visibly, but although the same thought had occurred to me, I shamed him with some adolescent taunt and we continued digging in the artificial glare of our torches.

About four feet down, we were sweating from our labours and paused to rest. A hoot-owl hollered from a nearby tree, causing us both to jump, all the more so when an answering cry came from the far side of the field, then another and another.

'Goldarnit, Johnny, I'm scared. Owls don't go hootin' like they're in a choir.' Larry looked on the point of desertion.

'They're just birds, Larry. Calm down. You don't believe in ghosts, do you?' I asked condescendingly.

He responded with an unconvincing grunt, but plied his spade nevertheless until, moments later, it scraped on something in the earth. He stopped abruptly, casting a wary glance at me; we were down deep now, standing in a short trench.

I reached up for a flashlight and shone it at his feet, a few inches from which something white reflected its beams. Larry stooped over and brushed the earth from a skull which grinned up at us. Joe's story had been true.

Even as he touched the hideous object, there was another chorus from the owls and a whirring of wings overhead.

'God Almighty, I'm gettin' outta here!' cried my friend, hauling himself out of our excavation, and dashing off into the night. His spade lay where it fell, beside the skull. He ignored my calls for him to return and was quickly lost in the pitch dark night.

Although the temptation to follow his example was great, I steadied my nerves and knelt down, scraping the dirt from the rest of the bones, for a complete skeleton was indeed there. Overhead I could hear birds fluttering and hooting. It was chillingly bizarre; birds, even owls, are just not that active at night, but I told myself that our antics, particularly Larry's melodramatic flight, had disturbed them.

The wooden handle had long since rotted way, but there it was, beside one set of skeletal fingers, a beautiful stone axe-head, as perfect when I touched it as it was when my great-great-grandfather buried it with the man he had shot dead. I held it a minute, then without conscience slipped it into my pocket.

Shifting more earth soon revealed some beads, once on a string, perhaps a leather thong, but now loose in the soil about his neck.

They were actually quite unimpressive, and I would have left them, but the glint of metal caught my eye and I fished out from the vertebrae a silver coin which quickly joined the artefact already in my pocket.

I had no idea what time it was – boys did not possess watches of their own in those days before teenagers were invented – but it struck me that dawn would soon be breaking. I had to be home in bed, but first I had to leave the field as I found it.

I had been careful not to disturb the remains, and, checking that no further 'treasures' were in evidence, I began to shovel the heaped earth back in on top of the Indian. It was easier and quicker than uncovering him but I was constantly distracted by the owls whose cacaphony had by now reached a crescendo. The sounds of wings in the darkness seemed all around me, but though I spun about, I never saw a single bird.

At last it was filled in. It took considerable will-power to stop to replace the sods we had carved out, but to neglect that would have ensured exposure. I finished the job and half-ran, half-walked back to the farm house, where I discreetly regained my bed-room and surprisingly fell fast asleep, only to be shaken awake by my mother after what seemed to be only seconds. The chores had to be done, sleepless night or not. Even today, I wake up at dawn despite my flexible working day as a journalist. It sometimes can be useful, too.

Nevertheless, that night was the last peaceful sleep I had for long enough.

I saw Larry the next day and showed him the axe-head, which he admired keenly. I kept quiet about the coin, however, for reasons I did not fully understand, even now. He was disappointed over the beads but took my word that they were no loss; he clearly felt that his desertion left him no entitlement to the spoils, so there was no diminution in our friendship.

It was fairly soon that the first misfortune befell our farm, when a fire mysteriously broke out in the hen house, killing twenty chickens before we could put it out.

Only a week later the new tractor toppled over and my father escaped serious injury by the narrowest of margins, while in November we lost one of our best cows through some normally routine ailment. Christmas was sad that year, because Uncle Joe was taken to hospital. A common cold had laid him low and to our doctor's bafflement he deteriorated overnight and died on New Year's Day. It was a cruel winter.

All this time, the trophies from the Ojibway grave had lain in my secret hiding place at the back of the barn, where I kept my other prized possessions too. Every so often, I would sneak off and bring them out, fondling the stone weapon and studying the coin. With the help of the town library, I had identified it as of French origin, struck in the reign of Louis XIV. It confirmed my belief that its bearer had been a chief, inheritor of a talisman handed down from predecessors who had battled the first incursions of the Europeans and despoiled them of their wealth. All this time, too, my nights had been troubled by odd, unwholesome dreams, in which a weirdly familiar landscape was haunted by shadowy figures, while owls hooted in the trees. It was the trees that dominated the scene, dense towering forests, yet somehow the terrain was within my ken. Night after night, I woke in the wee small hours, only to have the dream-fright continued by owlish noises beyond the dark bulk of the barn.

A sudden thaw led to the cellar being flooded in February, ruining my mother's vast supply of preserves, while March was heralded by the painful death of my dog in a road accident.

I was not raised to be superstitious, but even my strictly Presbyterian elders had begun to talk of the 'judgement' on our household, though how they could imagine their innocuous life-style had merited such misfortune, Lord knew.

But then I fell ill, just a fever, my folks said when it first hit me. But it went on and on, easing off now and then but returning each time with increased force. The town doctors were at a loss to explain it.

I was frequently delirious but even now I remember how the realisation came, one morning while my parents sat in prayer beside my bed, seeking deliverance from what had befallen us. It was not a dream, I swear it even now, but more a sudden fading of the room and a picture, like a movie, superimposed on the domestic scene. The forest of my nightmares, clearer than ever before, and standing still within it, a near naked bronzed figure, carrying a stone-headed axe and wearing a silver coin around his neck. Matted black hair and gaudy smears across his face could not deny the nobility of his countenance, as he gazed at me solemnly, then pointed at the ground beneath his feet.

At once I knew; that spot was the dark patch in the corn, some sacred square set in the primeval woods which had covered our fields and all Ontario in those far-off days. He was telling me that he could not – would not – rest – or let me rest – until he was restored to his rightful dignity.

The vision faded. Was it a dream, I wondered, as I focused again on my anxious father's face? I stopped wondering as I felt a strength I had not known for weeks. I was well. I sat up and asked for food, to my parents' delighted surprise. But I knew what had to be done, although I could not that day prevail against maternal dedication and had to stay in bed.

The night afterwards, however, I was out at midnight, spade clutched tightly in one hand, axe-head and coin secure in my pocket, having rescued them from my secret store that afternoon. Without Larry's help, it took me much longer, but I unearthed those old bones for a second time, again with a constant ululation from the owls, and, carefully and reverently, I replaced the coin and the axe-head, then filled in the earth once more.

There was a kind of sigh as I patted the topsoil back in place, which you might maintain was the wind in the thin line of trees down the side of the field. I thought more along the lines of that older forest, from my dream.

I walked back down the dirt-road, my ears alert for something I couldn't pin down. The silence! The night was devoid of the hooting cries of the owls, which I had heard every hour of darkness since Larry and I had done the deed all those months ago. Of course, adolescents have vivid imaginations, but one thing was for sure.

We suffered no further grief. I don't know if the Indian had laid a curse on us or not, but a strange thing happened shortly afterwards.

You may recall the big tornado that hit Ontario that spring. It came right up past Stratford, did a lot of damage everywhere it touched on. It arrived in our vicinity two days after I replaced the Indian's possessions and in its whirlwind pattern it cut a swathe which tore off the McDonalds' barn roof, uprooted the Harveys' orchard, flattened the Crowthers' pig-pen and killed Pete Afton by whipping his wagon over on top of him. Every single farm on every side of ours was harmed one way or another. But the tornado never so much as pitched over a fence-post on our land.

Another thing. I read a lot about Indians after that. Especially the Ojibway. They worshipped owls. Sacred guardians, they called them, who warded off evil and watched over the spirits of the dead.

That green patch was still there last summer when I drove past the proud old farm. The new owners had a boy aged around twelve and he looked a lively kid. Better to let sleeping bones lie, so we never let on about the greener patch in the middle of the back field.

IX

Warm as Snow

Mike Sims

She had hair of snow, ice skin, the smile of a frozen wind. She was the Snow Queen and he worshipped her. I knew that and it made my grief easier to bear when she came for him. Nothing was able to comfort me except knowing the final victory was waiting.

If the glare of unwelcome public attention made my emotions seem naked, my sorrow was held in check so I could gaze upon it, try to draw strength from its alienation. When his funeral was prepared I helped the best I could, but my mind was elsewhere. I was certain of only one thing. I would never sell the house. Its memories were my only ally, as much for ammunition as for comfort. Had I really the coldness to fight? Could I forget or would I in turn become the Snow Queen?

The pattering feet of the rain trampled over the mourning black we had all bought for the burial. For the family to be united was a cause for celebration of sorts. Black clothes were seeping wet from the hearse black clouds which hovered overhead for a look at the dead, a glance at the commiserative carrion who herded in the mud at the graveside. Skeletons of trees, like gangling choirboys, stood with heads bowed from the weight of rain rather than fear or respect. A harsh winter wind, with the clarity of the innocent, whisked the pale remaining drifts of snow into the air, away from the melting rain, brushed them against us, breaching our defences like the words of the minister.

I saw my sister whisper to her husband and then look over at me and smile the strained understanding compassionate smile people use at funerals. The discomfort of the others was plain, their minds obviously filled with the fact that their bodies were wet. I began to cry suddenly and silently, the tears rolling down my face mixing with the grim rain.

*

He woke to snow.

Before his eyes were open he knew there was snow. He lay in bed in the warm room in darkness and he knew. The window was covered with the grey film of moisture slowly trickling onto the narrow window ledge, seeping into the hem of the drapes half pulled away from the glass. The moisture told him the snow had arrived, uninvited, unannounced, unwelcome.

With the sly entrance of the unwanted guest, eyes appraising every corner for possible detection, the snow was upon him, and with it, the fear. The months of peace were at an end as though they had never been.

The air in the room was stale, the window had remained tightly shut since the first hint of snow some weeks before. The doors too were locked, and the edges and sides taped to prevent draught or moisture creeping in. Yet it was the front door he heard creak open and an envelope flutter to the floor.

Motionless he lay in the bed, his eyes screwed shut, his breathing slow and gentle to produce no sound. The air around him clogged with silence and the sour smell of disuse. He listened for the footfall near the stair, the sound of breathing not his own. The bedside clock was loud. He had to listen past its incessant beat. The slightest movement from his body made the sheets rustle like a thousand people shouting together. So he stayed still until the force of his controlled breathing became too strong and he breathed, almost choked, a single cry. Immediately he flinched against the pillow drawing his legs to his chest, pulling the bedspread across for flimsy protection. Unnecessary protection. The room remained empty.

*

I think it was a cousin who placed his arm about me and murmured. The words of the service became more remote.

The uncontrollable rain was beating on the coffin, drowning the words, making them superfluous, stating that tears were not enough.

The rain became impossible to ignore. It was the centre of concentration. The words, the feelings, sadness, dawning fear, recurrent loneliness, were inferior to the physical discomfort.

I leaned heavily on the male cousin allowing him to make the mistake that I needed his comfort. He responded by increasing his pressure around me, responding in the involuntary way natural to him. I knew that though it was not a deliberate thought his mind was instructing him to seduction. The subconscious action to flirt, to increase the pressure of his charm, make advances even though he may be happily married, even though he may be at the funeral of a relation, even though the woman is the widow.

My wedding day was perfect. Spring was gentle with early mornings lolling through the winter haze until I was waking to the sun and spending evenings with it. The day was warm with enough wind to raise the hem of the dress from the ground and make the posed photo session a lengthy affair. I was never so happy.

*

The stale air was still. When he opened his eyes there was no change. The snow remained. His mind filled with blues and yellows, golden and brown, but he knew the suffocating white was all around. Thought was no escape.

His breathing became regular. He stared at the bare wall opposite the bed, not hoping for courage but for salvation. How often he had imagined this time, thought of what he might do, might think, of the alternatives there might be. How wrong he had been. He felt too tired to move, disinclined to throw back the false cover, to enter the waking world.

There was not the abstract fear he imagined. He stayed calm. He had always felt it to be inevitable and that helped. There was no surprise, which would have added panic to the controlled tension rising in him.

It was bright outside, the whiteness causing the curtains to appear transparent as the morning light tried to insinuate into the room to join in his despair, heralding and shouting the snow. There remained an intrigue; something, a letter, had been delivered and waited on the doormat. It was painful to rise, to place a foot on the hard, dry carpet. The room was a comfort with its warmth, its insularity, its firmness. The windows were wet, it was true, but the cause was the snow, not running inside the house but making its dampness spread through the glass. The walls were sound. The chimney too was safe, the bricked up fireplaces would hold out the cold snow although the insistent flakes were probably resting even now on the bricks, unable to find a way in. If only he had thought to board the windows, or at least those downstairs, where drifts might build and force entry.

*

The honeymoon was glorious with weather we had no right to expect for the season. We drove down. I asked to share the driving but he would not hear of it and so I navigated from the passenger's seat although I think I was rather superfluous as he seemed to know exactly where he was going. The sun shone the whole way, but I took little notice of the scenery. It was too early for scenic colour, with a few patches of shrubs standing amongst the earth brown grasses. Winter moisture was evident in the pools which would be dried by the summer heat to leave bare hollows where grasses might intrude or animals might shelter from the sun. He seemed intent with concentration on the road, with little interest in the damp beauty of the passing scene.

We were going to spend the week in a little town on the coast. I glimpsed it first through the trees as we wound down into the valley. Then we took a corner and the town was there, laid out in front with a stone bridge across a fast flowing shallow river. The dips and winds of the road had shown us only part of the scene. In total it was splendid.

The hotel was quiet, out of season. How silly of that maid to imagine my husband could be interested in her, and on his honeymoon. She claimed he asked her into our room when all the time she was scheming to find a time when I was taking a walk in the town. She made quite a fuss.

*

Once up it was tempting to look out from the window. He knew what he would see. The snow would be thick. Trees would bow under the weight of cones of snow, the flowers and plants would be flattened. Grass would be white, unbroken, stretching like the sea from a beach, melting into the horizon, which was also white.

With the whiteness would be the peculiar silence that comes with snow. The silence of more than peacefulness, of more than solitude, the silence of waiting. The crisp coolness in the air would hold undimmed patience, as though straining to hear a whisper which was always fading too soon. There might be a wind, a mild flutter of the light fresh surface snow, lifting it a few inches in a flurry, or a biting wind which carried the cruelness to rip through the thickest coat and scrape the flesh.

He dressed slowly, taking care with each item, as if the action was new to him or his appearance was important. He was unable to lose the feeling that he was being watched over his shoulder. When he finished dressing he tossed the cover back onto the bed, sealing in the crumpled sheets and the dry warm safety. The room had a suspicious chill to it prompting him to think invasion was already achieved. He was drawn to the window and the view. No amount of shifting ornaments or prolonged combing of hair would disguise the desire to prevent the inevitable.

The room was almost as light as day now with the curtains drawn. There was no real need to open them, especially if he was going downstairs. He stood before the curtains realising fear was futile.

*

At last the service ends with a shrug and the minister turns aside, leaving the gaping hole with the rain pouring in for the onlookers to cherish. My mother is brave, holding my father's arm for appearance's sake, wearing her funeral perfume to match her delicate outfit. His mother breaks down of course, but then she could do little else. I have cried and meant it. Now the spontaneity is gone. The crowd shuffles away towards the dry cars, with the promise of food and drink to follow. The male cousin coughs and rejoins his wife, no doubt chalking another moral victory. I am the last to leave the graveside after sprinkling some soaked earth onto the grave. Like scuttling beetles the cars are already filing from the gates.

From the street the cemetery has the appearance of neat little markers, set to one side of the crumbling church, between bushes and trees. Strings tied around thin sticks in the ground mark fresh plots. The wind picks the bare bones of the trees, shaking them like river reeds whistling a plaintive note. My limousine is the last to leave, purring with sated luxury on superior feet. At mother's house the talk will have begun around the oil-fired radiators to the sipping of small drinks and the gnawing of sandwiches. Thin women with damp nylon dresses sticking to their inadequate bodies will converse with vague relations developing a sniffle. Large men with telephone voices talk loudly about possessions while thinking about heart attacks.

'No, really, I always watch it even if some of them are reruns. I never saw it the first time around you see.'

'What does your broker suggest for long term?'

'I think she looks ill. Took it very well, yes, but you can see how it's affected her.'

I drifted from one group to another accepting their sympathy and refilling empty glasses. Some avoided me as if embarrassed to speak, others made a point of being seen to commiserate, endorsing their humanity. After a short while the male cousin and his wife come to apologise because they have to leave early. She has developed a headache.

*

Outside there was only whiteness. Snow had stopped falling. The pavement was covered, indistinguishable from the street or the grass. The low stone wall around the garden was hidden. The roof of the nearest house was white. Scratched into the white were wild patterns caused by the feet of frightened birds. There were no footmarks leading to the house.

The window was sound despite the moisture. With the electric fire the room would remain warm. The door was locked shut, another barrier to be broken. The key in the lock turned easily and the door pulled open. The landing was dark with furtive shadows glancing up as the boards creaked. He crept to the top of the stairs, the invading draughts slipping into the bedroom to take advantage of his absence. The room seemed dim in aspect, borrowing dark corners from the landing to confuse and disorientate.

The stairs were steep but the landing was a box of locked doors with one entrance of betrayed welcome. Each stair sounded a separate signal as he trod on it. He dared not touch the banister which was wooden and cold. Warily he reached the bottom step where he stood. There on the carpet beneath the front door was a letter. An addressed letter, hand-written, with no stamp.

*

'How are you going to manage now, without him I mean? Sorry that sounds a bit blunt, doesn't it?'

'Realistic.'

'Yes, but it must be hard to come to terms with surely?'

'It was a physical shock, of course, finding him like that, not as if I had warning.'

'What about the children?' She was my sister, with me cornered next to the tropical fish tank for a warm chat. Her husband, successful in his own business, was wiping off the soft drink that their smallest had just thrown over the couch.

'I haven't seen them for some time.'

'I noticed they didn't come today.'

'They may not know, I certainly didn't tell them.'

'But surely ...?'

'They were his children not mine. His first wife had access and made good use of it, they didn't have a good word for me.'

Mother came round with a fresh plate of sandwiches, 'All right, dears? ... You'll stay here tonight of course ... no look you will ... your father will have a word.'

Sister took two sandwiches and concentrated on the texture of the bread.

'You surely didn't think it was normal that he was in the house alone?' I said.

'I thought you had gone away for a few days.'

'A few more than that.'

'You mean the, I mean, his death saved, or prevented rather ...?'

'Death instead of divorce, you mean?'

She pretended to find the bread fascinating again. Father loomed out of the corner of my eye to persuade me to spend the night with them. I wasn't really sure if I wanted to go back to the house or not. I had not been there for several weeks and the thought of staying there alone was depressing somehow, despite my strong resolve. I was determined to keep the house, and to keep it intact. Intact with all its oddities and secrets, all the mysteries which he could never discover but which uncovered him. I knew all the shadows he flinched from, all the corners he could only partly see, all the cries and pains he could not hear. All he heard, all he saw, all he felt, was his own imperfection. He tried to fight back, the poor man.

*

He fingered the letter, recoiling at the sharp coldness of the paper as if it were brittle ice. The envelope was addressed in blue ink in tiny lettering. Inside was a single sheet of paper. 'Thank you for your invitation, I will be calling today.' No signature.

The Snow Queen. He knew enough not to be surprised. She would come and enter. After all his preparations she would beat him. The letter was only the first scar of defeat. Where had he lost? Or had he ever begun to win? He remembered the battles, the skirmishes, the moments of truth. His could be viewed a long term defeat, concealed in deceits and embellishments. The gradual wearing down, the erosion of one value to be replaced by another, until she was left with only confusion and he with arrogance in place of guilt.

He could remember a happy snow, one Christmas, when there was no fear in throwing and rolling the snow, walking home with arms wrapped around each other, not noticing that this kept them warm as well. Feeling the lacy flakes on his face, catching them on his tongue to eat them before they melted. She was small and delicate, yet strong when he chased her across the grass and holding her they kissed without fuss. Then the snow brought them together. Now today, it would again, but there would be no time to catch the snow on his tongue.

Upstairs could now be sealed off, he was not going to be safe there again. Snow may have blown into the attic, perhaps that was why it was so quickly vulnerable. The wind sounded loudly outside, whipping into a frenzy, rattling the door in its frame, shaking the windows. It was near. Fresh snow flicked against the glass smearing the clearness.

The kitchen door was shut, forbidding him to open it. The door to the front room was shut but not locked. This was the room he had last been in and where he felt most safe. He screwed the letter with the envelope and put them in his pocket. When he turned the handle of the door he thought he heard something shuffle away inside. The room was empty when he entered, a smell of his tobacco lingered but suffused with it was a sweet scent like roses after rain, or evening honeysuckle.

The room was ordinary enough, each chair exactly as he had left them, the book on the coffee table, the armchair drawn to the fire, the glass on the arm, the bureau flap open with a pen and paper ready. Yet there was an atmosphere. Something had been displaced. He sat in the chair flicking the pages of the book and was not able to remember what it was about. Distress was uppermost, the need to distinguish the commonplace from the unusual, to realise which shadow was darkest, which object was moved, which truth to mistrust. It was too cold in the room. Then he noticed, the window was open, the tape was broken and blowing in the draught.

*

More people were leaving now, squeezing my hand and smiling. Others were still drinking, mulling over sandwiches and platitudes, comparing clichés and successes. My sister was talking to mother, no doubt jointly abhorring my attitude, condemning me for being callous. Yet I had never flaunted faithfulness, or even attempted to hide the problems from them. They chose to ignore, or were unable to prevent themselves from ignoring, the warning cries.

'We must go now, dear, the kids to feed.'

'They're at home?'

'With a neighbour, thought we'd better not bring them, you know.'

'Thanks for coming then.'

The house was bitterly cold when I found him. The door wide open, drifts of clean snow, white over the carpet. The only fire was in the bedroom with condensation dripping from the walls, the windows were taped shut. The other doors were all locked, except the front room, where I found him.

Snow was a catalyst to his moods I always found, although it took a few winters to realise. Strangely he seemed to look forward to the colder weather, he always said the autumn was his favourite time, when the anticipation was most intense and the pleasure could not be spoiled by disappointment. His joy was derived from planning, the event never quite fulfilling his hopes. Later I grew impatient of his obsession with draughts and moisture of any kind. The house became so airless in winter that I developed headaches which gained no sympathy.

She had loved the snow.

I felt her presence as soon as I entered. It was just as strong as it had been at first, when I lived in the house after we married. I knew he was haunted by her but that was surely natural. What was not natural and what I resented but could never explain to him was her presence in the house. That was uncalled for. He of course was totally blind to my feelings. When I suggested a redecoration he argued, when I wanted ornaments moved he disagreed, and he would move them back later thinking I didn't notice. Perhaps now I could persuade her to stay if she was still there.

*

There was no need to close the window now, there was nothing left to keep out except the cold and he was too late for that. The room was full, the curtains blowing, paper rustling, glasses on the shelves rattling against each other like frozen teeth. His breath misted in front of him, mirroring the snow rushing in through the window to lie on the carpet and furniture. He had waited for this moment for years, and feared it as well. There was none of the grandeur of the finale he might have expected, no feeling of elation, nor of revelation. Instead there was an emptiness of emotion. His clothes were drenched and clung to his body like a pleading prisoner. The snow invaded the corners of the room, replacing the shadows which faded into memory. A whirling wind filled the room with shouts and curses, sorcerers' spells, revenge from the woman he had expected, the woman the snow had made possible. His body felt angular, awkward, a mere spectator to events.

The snow was over his feet, melting yet still building in depth. A woman's voice was in the room, calling his name, stating his case, condemning him. There was no warmth at all in the voice, none in the room. He sank to his knees under the weight of consciousness, the weight of sudden truth. He felt no mercy and there was none to be given.

The snow was over his feet, and as he knelt, the snow covered his body, easing into his mouth, closing his eyes, laying him down to rest. The snow.

*

I found him in the front room, the window wide, the last of the snow blowing in. The books were torn to shreds, the chairs clawed, the wood chipped and broken. He lay on his side the clothes ripped from him, the skin frozen in more than the stiffness of death, frozen by the unnatural cold into an opaque hardness. The footprints on the front path and lawn were wildly irregular, many feet jumbled together like dancers.

The grave is overgrown at the moment, I never seem to have as much time to tend to it as I should wish. The house keeps me busy, cleaning and dusting trying to keep it proper for her. The front room is always cold, even in summer. And in the winter a draught laughs through the windows despite the precautions I take. I feel so safe there I have no need to worry about the snow. Last year I left a window or two open when it snowed and it collected on the sill, but I was happy. The snow settles contentedly on the grave, I know it has no reason to disturb me. I remain faithful.

I have no complaint. He quarrelled, not I.

X

Meeting Mr Singleton

Derek Stanford

October 12, 1946: A curious old man spoke to me today. He had seen me, apparently, wearing my khaki when I first came to Lincoln's Inn Fields on Tuesday. He asked me, very courteously, if I was on leave, or awaiting my discharge. I told him I had got my papers in my pocket, that I had worn my hospital blues so long (how many plastic reconstructions of my skull, how many weeks in rehabilitation centres!) that I thought I'd revert to battle-dress for just a few days before junking it for ever. He smiled and seemed to like my ritualistic sense, and we chatted on in leisurely fashion. What I did not tell him was that I found in khaki a sort of cover. It was just the no-man's-land kind of dress for someone not knowing where he belonged – for someone unable to say quite who he was.

I learnt that once he had read for the Bar, had fought in the Great War, suffered from shell-shock, and never entirely recovered from it. He said he believed we were predisposed to things like getting wounded or getting married. Was I married? Well, yes, I was, I answered. 'Then you are doubtless predisposed to it,' he said.

October 13: I was having coffee at a green iron table which they serve from a kiosk in among the trees when once more the old man came over and talked to me. All about himself. I listened: I had nothing else to do.

October 14: Three more days to make a decision, and here I sit watching as the tennis courts empty and the gardeners ignite their first sacrifice of leaves. From small dun pyramids the curdled smoke rises, seeking slow egress from the smouldering core. Where does my own true spark lie buried, or am I to consume like sick green wood in acrid clouds without conflagration?

October 15: The old man has invited me round for a drink. His name is Singleton. He owns a house in Red Lion Square, the top half of which, I gather, he lets. So long as there's room for my books, he says, they can swing me with the cat. The neighbourhood in general is one I remember from my own discontinued days in the Law, which is why, perhaps, I have returned to it while waiting. I am seeking to articulate the laws of my own nature. It is this, together with a curious apprehension concerning my visit to Singleton tonight (as if some revelation awaited me there), which leads me to set out in black and white the strange story of my relations with C –. When I have detailed it in full perhaps I shall see the situation like a corpse on a table prepared for an autopsy.

In the early days of the war when I was billeted near Cambridge, C – sought me out with tactful persistence. I had known her in London before the war as a friend of friends and seen her at parties. Now she was engaged in war-work in Cambridge and her brother (her junior by two years) was reading history at Queen's.

It was, in fact, to his rooms that she first invited me to tea on learning of my whereabouts in the neighbourhood. Seeing sister and brother together, I was astonished by their double beauty: she so dark and he so fair – a corn-gold god in pink shirt and green cords. Of course, I had always been aware of her brunette good looks and allure; but, beside her young brother, the impact of her charms seemed strengthened. Off-set and balanced, as it were. I thought of them in my mind together; wondering, now I had seen them both, how they achieved a separate existence.

What my imagination could not envisage, experience soon realized for me. It was not long before C – was saying she had two tickets for a concert. Debusey and Ravel – they were favourites with me, weren't they? I, for my part, would rather have been in a punt with the two of them on the Cam than in an auditorium on a warm early-summer night.

But C – had the ability to hold my attraction by making me more aware of myself. She encouraged and appealed to the actor in me, so that in her presence I was constantly acting out a drama with myself at the centre. She kept the spotlight of attention off herself in a deft and subtle manner: not by any reticence or reserve but rather by putting all her energy into providing an audience – one which elicited, applauded and supported the other figure upon the stage.

Then, too, I was taken by her capacity to share the things I brought her: information, anecdotes, statements and opinions. Her signalled excitement of lips and eyes – these tokens stimulated and impressed me. Also she asked me no personal questions unless I made clear that the territory was open. She chose to place herself under my spell; and, though she showed herself responsive, made no demands, suggested no commitments.

One Saturday night late in May when the girl friend who shared a small house with her on the outskirts of the town was away for the weekend, C – invited me to dinner. Prior to this we had been drinking with her brother in a pub in Mill Lane. While we had sat on the parapet of the bridge by the mill-race with mugs of cider in our hands, C – had said to him, with easy casualness which yet preserved the tones of self-revelation: 'You know, I find I'm getting very fond of Richard.' 'And so am I, and so am I,' replied her brother, giving me a gentle gold-leaf smile.

What more natural, then, that after coffee and a liqueur, I should help her wash up and carry her upstairs to bed. As we lay by turns awake and asleep, she was all accommodating clinging caresses. It was I, next day, who suggested we be married.

From this time forward, she saw to it that the two of us and her brother were together as little as possible. He was going down in the second week of June and joining the RAF. There was not all that time for us to consort. And when we had told him of our plans, he had congratulated us and smiled, but his smile seemed to carry a sorrowful shadow. 'How I shall miss you, both of you!' he murmured. And then, 'We shall all of us miss each other soon.'

His words appeared to me to promise something more than a general doom – the loss by absence of friends and lovers in war-time. It was as if they hinted at some special fate to be visited on the loves of us three – an intimation later realized. Then, too, as between him and myself, there was some tie I hardly understood. It was not when I was with brother and sister, but alone with C – that I felt its fascination – a pull which somehow delighted and puzzled, and then appalled me. Sometimes when I was looking at C – – not, as it were, to examine her features but just to hold her face before me as I talked – it was his image that loomed to meet me, not optically but in the mind's eye. I seemed to see his eyes listening to me.

Nor was that the limit of the manner in which some part of my nature was haunted by his looks – his face, his body. As at the climax of our first love-making, C – momently closed her eyes, it was his countenance I beheld for one long second on the pillow. The morning after I had slept late. Surfacing from sleep, with my eyes still closed, I sensed someone bending over me. It was C – in a gold dressing-gown bringing me a cup of tea; but before I opened my eyes – in a dream was it or a wakened memory? – I seemed to see her brother standing by the bed, naked save for a pair of shorts as when I had seen him on the banks of the Cam, his tanned torso and golden chest-curls glistening in the sun that day we had gone bathing. These hallucinations were the more disturbing since I had never before questioned the direction of my sexual instincts.

By the time we were married, her brother had joined the Air Force and been posted. He was unable to attend the ceremony at the Register Office; and, as if his absence affected us, our relationship changed right from the start. Whereas, before our marriage, C – had subdued her personality to mine and taken an initiative only on my promptings, she now began to concentrate her interest and attention upon herself. In a sense, she became forgetful of me, not as a physical presence (of which she was most alertly aware) but as a being with developed thoughts and feelings different and distinct from her own.

We had only five days of married life together since I was called back to my unit which was about to embark for Africa. Nor was I sorry to be called away. The bright companion who had reflected back each of my moods as if a faithful mirror now became a lamp, so to speak, with a hard concentrated light all its own. In bed or up and about, this change in her was manifest.

Oh, but this was not what I had intended! How could I have known that the soft odalisque, whom I thought I had discovered in C –, was the furious maenad I had married? Being legally given over to her, I felt her lay hands on me as if I was there to be devoured. She did not experience me as a person, she took me for the four elements. I was fire to warm her; water to quench her; earth to sustain her; air, around her, to assimilate and breathe. She thought I was like the festive trees whose boughs could be stripped to form an awning over her head. She imagined me like a running stream into which she plunged to refresh herself. I hear her voice as she put back my hand, as one might put back a strand of weed which interferes with one's drinking the clear water of a stream: 'Lie still,' she ordered, her thighs crouched over me.

It was not that I could not cope with her demands, but rather that the supremacy which she had accorded me was at one stroke withdrawn. I was not now the striker but the gong. I remember her saying to me one morning in bed, 'You're really feminine – like my brother.' In truth, I no longer recognized C – as the woman I had known before marriage. Neither did I trust or recognize myself. The recall to my unit came as a relief. What did the ancients say of Africa – that some new monster could always be relied upon to emerge from it? I was leaving *my* monster to sail for its shores.

Old history this! Where lies the future? Two more days to make a decision; and tonight I can see only as far as Red Lion Square.

October 16: Strange what madness urbanity can hide! For, of course, Singleton is mad; diseased with some terrible obsession. What other explanation could there be of it? And yet, that corroborating picture he showed me? Painted, he said – and certainly dated – before it all, in 1899. But what does a rural landscape painting prove? 'The Bower of Leaves, Oak House, Wykehamsted.'

'Insane,' I go on repeating, but cannot escape the

foreknowledge, the clairvoyance of the tale he told me; how all the elements of my own story were fused and shadowed forth in his. And that obscene multi-image at the centre.

I arrived at Singleton's about eight o'clock. His rooms were smaller than I had expected, but fine and cared for; his library fascinating. We sat in a shelf-filled mirror-hung apartment with two white rugs, soft and close as snow. A magnificent collection of volumes beckoned to me. The Romantics mostly, English and German, both major and minor authors represented. An attractive odd selection of modern writers too. Few eighteenth-century titles, and little Greek or Latin.

It was as the brandy warmed our vision (though I noticed I was drinking more sparingly than Singleton) that he offered to tell me a story – a true story, *his* story he insisted. It belonged, he said, to the pre-war period. To the days before the Great War when I was young.

His prologue was clearly intended to provide him with any licence he required. It excused him from too many questions. Nothing mad in such a gambit.

In 1900, he told me, he was twenty, a Balliol undergraduate and heir to a country house and wooded estate. The property was at Wykehamsted in Berkshire into which his father had moved that autumn while he himself was up at Oxford. The memories of the old are passionate but patchy, without proper sequence. And his tale itself was such a farrago of sick-room brooding and unattested gossip that I must excuse any lacunae, any slips on the ladder of cause and effect. He poured another brandy and continued.

During the Christmas vacation, in 1900, he had gone down with rheumatic fever. His father was barely settled into their new home before he was off to South Africa with his yeomanry regiment to fight the Boers. Singleton's own mother was dead; and so, save for an ancient aunt, there was no one in the house except servants, some of these being new faces to him. In these circumstances, it was not unnatural that his illness should have been cheerless and protracted.

One long yellow February day young Singleton ventured out, in his convalescence, for a walk in the grounds. He was stopped by a woodman, someone he did not recollect, who advised him on no account to take the short cut through

Flora's Dell. There was something being bred there which mustn't be disturbed. The fence surrounding the Dell had partly blown down, but Singleton was told: 'The Dell should be given a wide berth.'

The afternoon moon had already risen over the wood when Singleton turned for home. His way led through a dense plantation; and so far he had observed the woodman's words, though with some scepticism as to their necessity. But now, from his walk, he was overcome with tiredness, and therefore decided upon the short cut.

'Woodman or no woodman ...' I can still hear his words, as he sat binding me in his madness like the Ancient Mariner. Here is the language in which he told his story, as nearly as I can recall it:

Halfway through Flora's Dell, an indefinite scent caused him to halt, to sniff the air and turn about, seeking for its source. It was not a tree-smell, fern-smell, or turf-smell – no smell he had previously encountered in the wood. Neither was it one of those artificial smells which he had met with about the house: the ancient aroma of cigar-smoke, pipe-smoke, women's perfume. Nor did it resemble smells of cooking. As it hung across his path, like a band invisibly suspended, it seemed somehow natural odour but one in which nature was quickened. As he stood to puzzle it out, it conjured up the wandering scents of summer. He thought of hawthorn, convolvulus, the smell of grass, and the breath of cows. So distinct was that illusion of a night in summer that he tore off the heavy ulster he was wearing. Then, shifting a pace to left or right, he sought to locate the direction of the scent. It appeared to be stretched in a positive band, like the width of some unseen material, and whereas to one side of the path he could barely detect it, on the other side it clung in the air about him with a breath-taking appeal.

In the receding daylight of the scene, with the moon's assistance, he dimly made out a hut or summer-house in among the trees. As he moved towards it, the scent continued, as if this arbour might be its source. On a nearer viewing, the shelter showed itself a kind of rudimentary bower, half artificial yet completed by nature. Some sort of simple trellis-work appeared to constitute three sides of a roof, but over this creepers and brambles had twisted in a tangled fibrous profusion. The fourth side, affording a door or entrance, was open to the air, and all inside was empty save for a great mound of leaves on the floor. He stood mystified on the threshhold of this bower, his lungs and nostrils drunk with the scent which seemed to stream from the heaped-up leaves, and to quicken his consciousness to some eluding question, some evasive state of mind which brimmed his eyes with tears.

He took a step forward into the bower, the scent dinning hammer-wise in his brain. Distracted, he craned forward over the leaves, the perfume pouring up like smoke from below. Stumbling, he started to circle the mound, the scent drenchingly sweeter, intenser, when suddenly the floor was gone beneath him, the earth swallowed him. He fell through blackness, his consciousness eclipsed in his descent. When he revived, he found himself supported on the breast and lap of a furry-smelling *creature* ...

Can I continue with Singleton's tale? Can I bring myself to write down its full horror? O God, save me from this mental chaos, this blasphemy which somehow mirrors my confusion!

I have opened the door of my room, have let myself out in the empty street, have walked beneath the shining small-hour stars. I am calmer now, and curiously numb.

October 17: I have pondered this matter incessantly. Ridiculous that an old man's ruminations should have the power to sink my spirits, oppress my heart, and weigh down my conscience. Coincidence, I tell myself, and as for the tale, a romantic frenzy. I have seen my host's taste in books, have heard him speak of abortive attempts at writing, and can guess at his own frustrated talents. What, then, more likely than he should choose to fashion some wildly, fully private myth out of sick-room dreams? Rightly or wrongly, my chill imagination pursues and lives over Singleton's adventure.

I have spoken of what he recounted concerning a happening in his youth at about the turn of the century. No doubt he went to bed last night and forgot the story which stays so weirdly with me.

Singleton revived from his fall, from his fainting away through the up-rushing darkness, and found himself enfolded by a warm body whose pores were sweet with odours of the earth. His eyes and lids felt heavy with sleep; they were closing all the time of their own accord. Through the narrowing chink of sight, he discerned a shadowy den or cavern, filled with greyish light, and faced about with earthy walls. The creature who held his recumbent body half across its lap and against its breast, he could not see, being too weary to turn or move his gently-cradled head. But from the odoriferous softness of touch, he knew that his body must be in contact with the uncovered flesh of some warm-blooded thing. The lap across which he partly rested seemed broad, generous, and feminine, with thighs and loins like those of a woman. But against his neck, his ears, and skull he could feel the tickling texture of hair, of a masculine bosom abundantly covered. But could it be called masculine, since though the bone structure appeared to proclaim the male, two small mounded breasts carried other connotations? In any case, his mind was still dizzy, both from his fall and from the enveloping folds of scent which drooped about him in his prostration.

Then, just as his eyelids slipped down in sleep, a downy pad-like hand gently parted his half-open lips, while the other gently inserted between them a warm sweet-smelling nozzle of flesh like a supple elongated female nipple. Singleton's drifting senses swooned away in a vertigo of shuddering ecstatic revulsion. As his mind reeled in the turmoil of sensation, he felt the nerves of his throat alerted to receive a honied stream of milk like the juices of the earth poured out upon them.

For a period of time impossible to measure, Singleton lay in a sleeping-waking coma. And on those few occasions – minutes or hours? – when consciousness was fitfully restored, he would feel the touch of that firm furry breast, the accommodating warmth of those wide-spread thighs, the inebriating sweetness of that flowery dug so maternally thrust between his passive lips. Taste became smell; scent imagination. Mint, currant, parsley, thyme assailed the palate of Singleton's mind in separate relays and racing combinations. And in these giddy flights of awareness, he sensed the supporting strength of the creature whose tending of him seemed to cause it joy.

At length, came the time when his eyes opened to observe the protuberant roots of trees and the suckers of deeply-trailing plants showing through the rough earth sides of the cavern. His body was no longer roundly embraced by the flesh of the warm invisible being. Instead, he found himself with his back propped against the loamy walls of the cave. A greyish light whose source lay behind him made more apparent the dimensions of the chamber. The walls were about ten feet high, and steeply vertical with no marked footholds; but when he turned his head, a circle of moonlight appeared in a murky shaft above him. A nerve-cell awoke and flashed out the message 'Freedom'; and then the sweet lassitude of his drugged state floated him away on an apathetic tide. His senses, in memory, blossomed like flowers.

Again he was drifted to the shores of alertness; once more sucked back when consciousness relapsed. With a rhythm beyond his own determination, the process repeated itself without ceasing. Then, as he was washed for the umpteenth time, upon that beach of indefinite light, his vision fastened upon the roots of some protruding plant hanging like a life-line. Already he was feeling the sea's returning pull when his hand, unprompted it seemed by his will, stretched out and clutched the bunch of horny shoots. A little to the right, beyond his head, tuberous tufts of further roots clustered. Higher still, to the left, there were others, as if by design, these natural holds had been chosen to afford a way of ascent. In a frantic scramble, Singleton was up, his panting body resting on the edge of the shaft in a thicket within the Dell. Then he was running, gasping and sobbing, back through the gap in the blown-down fence, black clappers opening and shutting in his brain.

He was found on the evening of his disappearance, sick and moaning with a burning fever, by a gamekeeper whom the servants had alerted, having been made uneasy by his absence. It was seven o'clock when he was carried back to the house and put to bed with what was an obvious relapse in his condition. He had been missing only some two or three hours.

For a long time he lay seriously ill. His father was killed in South Africa, and he inherited the estate together with a small but competent fortune. He delayed taking his degree at

Oxford, and on obtaining it lived for some years a roving, restless, purposeless life. At length, he decided to read for the Bar. Before he was called, there came the Great War in which he volunteered and, as if by a wry confirmation of nature, was shell-shocked after being buried alive beneath the debris of a bombarded dug-out.

October 18: This is my last morning in Lincoln's Inn Fields. No sign of Singleton. His tale, however, keeps me company, having fatally attached itself to me. I ask myself is the story his or mine? What concerns, engages, and accuses is the identification which exists between this myth and my own divided life. The events narrated may not have taken place; but they have left their mark upon me.

At noon, I should be on the quay at Southampton to welcome a woman I have not seen for years. C – is returning from war-work in Canada. She expects to see me, but I shall not be there. Had her brother lived, it might have been different, but he was killed – shot down in his plane – six months after we were married.

*

This portion of a weather-stained uncompleted diary, found in a wood in Berkshire, was produced at a local Coroner's Court met to examine the cause of death of a young man whose body was discovered near by. The Coroner observed that the body had been found in what were once the grounds of Oak House, Wykehamsted, though the building had been burnt down in the 'thirties. Inquiries among residents of Red Lion Square, Holborn, as to any one who might have known the deceased, proved singularly unsuccessful. One recent death in that neighbourhood removed a possibly important witness.

The doctor who performed the post-mortem said there were signs of brain-deterioration which might have resulted from the extensive head-wounds the man had received during the war, though he thought the immediate determining cause was probably the icy Christmas weather to which the sick man had been subjected. Only one relation of the dead man was present, his wife Mrs Christine Child. The verdict given was Death by Exposure.

XI

The Neighbours

Meg Buxton

The door bell rang. Margaret woke from her light doze with a start and her thin fingers clutched the turned over edge of the bedclothes, her too-long nails rasping on the linen sheet: she must ask Jean to cut them for her, but not today; she was too tired.

Voices came from the hallway beyond the kitchen. Who was the visitor? No one to see her, she prayed: if it was, let Jean have the sense to tell them that she was not well enough to see anyone. The voices came nearer, her daughter's and – oh, no – not Vera Trevillian!

The door opened.

'Mother?' Jean approached the bed. 'Mrs Trevillian's come to sit with you for a little while. I've got to go and get Jonathan's uniform. He starts his new school tomorrow, you know.'

She looked down at her mother's gaunt face, the lines round her mouth and nose deeper than ever, the skin seeming to be stretched taut across the cheekbones and of a waxy paleness: the eyes were reproachful.

'I'm sorry, Mum,' she whispered. 'I won't be long. I'll tell her to sit in the living room, shall I? Ring the bell if you want her to get you anything.' She moved the small ornamental brass bell a little nearer her mother's hand and bent to kiss her cool cheek. 'I know you don't like her much, but I had to get someone. It'll be all right, though; I'll tell her not to come in unless you ring.'

It was too late. Vera was already in the room, the dining-room into which Jean had moved her mother's bed, her small dark eyes darting round, taking in the half-drawn curtains, the bunch of primroses in a mug which Jonathan had picked for his grandmother, the gas fire purring pinky-blue on the hearth, the bottle of pills on the table by the bed.

'You're never taking these green pills, are you, Margaret?' she demanded, picking up the bottle and reading the label with difficulty, screwing up her eyes with the effort.

'Oh, Mrs Trevillian!' Jean swung round. 'Mother's not feeling too good today, I told you. Look – I've made you a cup of tea –' she held out an arm, inviting the woman to leave the room, ' – and put it in the sitting room: the paper's there and some magazines. You'll be comfortable in there: leave the door open and Mother will ring if she wants anything.' But Vera Trevillian chose to ignore the young woman's anxious hints.

'Don't you worry, dear,' she said complacently. 'I've seen a lot of sickness in my time: I know what's wanted. I'll bring my tea in here, cheer your mother up a bit. But she never shouldn't be taking these pills.' She shook the bottle, making the contents rattle. 'The death of our Hilda, these were.'

'Please, Mrs Trevillian –!' Jean began, but a child's voice clamoured from the kitchen:

'Come on, Mummy!'

'Run along, dear,' Margaret whispered from the bed. 'I'll be all right. Off you go now, and good luck with the shopping.'

Jean hesitated. Her mother was desperately ill and she hated leaving her: it couldn't be long now, the doctor said, and every moment was precious. Usually she made sure that her elder sister or her brother's wife could come over before arranging to go out but today, like her, they were both busy getting their children ready for the start of the school term tomorrow. Vera Trevillian was the only person who could come at short notice and she was a kind old soul, bossy, but kind. Mother would be all right.

'Come *on*, Mummy!' the voice from the kitchen demanded again. 'We'll miss the bus!'

' 'Bye, Mum.' Jean smiled anxiously at the fragile figure in the bed. 'I shan't be long.' She shot a glance at Vera replacing the bottle of pills on the bedside table and jerking the folded-back sheet straight with an unmistakable air of being in charge. 'Don't tire her, please,' she implored. 'She honestly hasn't the strength to talk.'

*

Vera settled herself in the small arm-chair near the bed, her tea cup on the mantelshelf within easy reach. She crossed her legs at the ankle and turned her feet this way and that, one at a time, to admire her new black patent leather shoes: a bit wasted on present company, but you had to make a bit of an effort when you were going out, she told herself smugly. She tucked her bulging handbag in beside her and, having patted her rigidly-set iron grey hair and adjusted a string of purple beads, gave her skirt a final twitch from under her stout thighs and folded her arms across her ample bosom. Thus arranged she set about entertaining the invalid.

'Well, Margaret?' she started brightly. 'This will never do! How long is it now? Nearly three months you've been poorly, isn't it? I don't know what doctors is coming to these days: not like when we was young, is it? Bottle of tonic and we was right as rain in no time then, eh? All these pills don't do no good at all.'

Margaret smiled and shook her head weakly.

'Think they know everything, doctors do, and don't know nothing. I reckon I knows as much as what they do – more, prob'ly.' Vera's hand moved out towards the bottle of green pills again. 'These things, now,' she went on. 'Our Hilda was just like you: started with a little touch of flu, like: left to herself and a nice bottle of tonic from the chemist she'd of got over it, I said. But no: Wilfred said she had to have the doctor. Two of these green pills three times a day, he said, and – well, poor Hilda. A twelve-month next Friday it'll be since she went.' She put the pill bottle down again. 'I don't know what your Jean's thinking about, letting you take those, really I don't.'

There were some moments of blessed silence while Vera's eyes roved round the room. Old-fashioned stuff in here, she thought, taking in the Welsh dresser with its willow patterned plates in rows and the floral china tea service in front of them; the solid oak table pushed against the wall to make room for the bed and the wheel-backed chairs jammed into whatever space could be found for them. Liked a bit of modern stuff herself: nice bit of wipe-clean plastic she'd put on her table, and not a heavy old thing like this one it wasn't neither, but light and elegant with little slim pointed legs with brass on the ends, very pretty. And the curtains! You could get ever such dainty ones at the Co-op, ready made up, ever so nice they were, not like these heavy old velvet ones.

She lifted her tea cup and found it empty: there was more in the pot in the living room.

'Cup of tea in the other room,' she addressed Margaret, who lay with her eyes shut. 'Bring you one in, shall I?'

Margaret shook her head ever so slightly.

'No thank you,' she whispered.

Vera returned with her cup, stirring it noisily.

'Nothing like a cup of tea,' she said, sucking at the hot liquid. 'Sure you won't have one?'

There was no answer and she walked about the room, touching this and that disparagingly. She stopped by the window, wrenching the curtains wider apart – faded at the edges, she noticed; must be donkey's years old – and peered into the street.

'Nice day out,' she said conversationally. 'Rained last night, though – and the wind! Reminded me of the night our Hilda went. I said to my Wilfred, "Wilf," I said, "it was a night like this our Hilda went." Mind you, it was they green pills that was to blame; I've said so all along. "Wilf," I said, "if it wasn't for they green pills our Hilda would still be here." He said it was something else, like she was fading away, nothing to do with the pills, but I know different – oh!' She lent closer to the window pane. 'There's Doris! Doris Pendeen, you know Doris.' She banged on the glass. 'Doris! Doris! Come and see Margaret!' She beckoned energetically and then turned and crossed the room, her hips rolling with haste. 'Doris'll cheer you up,' she said, not looking at the figure in the bed. 'Proper scream, Doris is. I'll go and let her in.'

*

They sat, Vera and Doris, one each side of Margaret's bed, tea cups in hand.

'I fetched Doris a cup,' Vera informed the sick woman who lay with her eyes closed, her pale face drawn. 'You wouldn't begrudge Doris a cup of tea, would you?' she asked roguishly and rhetorically. 'No, of course you wouldn't.'

She smiled brightly at her friend across the bed.

'Well, what do you think of our patient, then?' she enquired, patting the thin fingers lying on the sheet and twitching out a wrinkle in the blanket with a proprietorial air. 'Proper picture, isn't she?' She made a wry face to make sure Doris didn't think she meant it.

Doris inspected the figure in the bed.

'Looks just like Jack's mother did before she went,' she said. Her eyes lit on the pill bottle. 'She's never taking those green pills, is she?'

'That's what I said!' Vera was triumphant. 'Isn't that just what I said?' she asked Margaret, in no way rebuffed at getting no answer. 'They green pills were the death of our Hilda: I'm surprised at Jean letting her take them, told her straight, I did, but I blame the doctor. Young Doctor James, she has, just like we had for Hilda, but I wouldn't have him no more, not after he was so rude to me. Some of the things he said! You'd never believe – neglect, he said, and after me waiting on her hand and foot –' She broke off abruptly, wishing she hadn't mentioned what the young doctor had said, but her friend hadn't been paying attention, being preoccupied with the pills.

'Jack's mother had these, too,' she said, examining the bottle. 'Didn't do her a bit of good.' She peered into her half empty cup. 'This tea's cold. Can't stand cold tea.'

Vera was on her feet in a moment.

'I'll make a fresh pot,' she said. 'Jean won't mind.'

'Better put in an extra spoonful,' Doris said, taking off her head scarf and pushing up her pinkish henna-ed hair. 'I met Connie Marshall as I was coming in. Told her I was going to see Margaret and she said she'd be in directly. She's been down to the sales.'

'That'll be nice,' Vera shrieked from the kitchen, clattering cups. 'She can show us what she got. I should be shopping, too, by rights, sales on and that, but – well, you've got to do a good turn when you can, haven't you?'

Doris shifted her skinny haunches uncomfortably on the hard seat of the wheel-backed chair Vera had pulled out for her and groped in her coat pocket for cigarettes and matches. No matches.

'See if you can find a match while you're out there, Vera,' she shouted. 'By the gas cooker, most likely.' She took her coat off and threw it on the end of the bed.

Margaret's eyes flew open, black in her ashen face, alarmed at the sudden weight on her legs.

'All right, love?' Doris asked loudly. 'Feeling a bit better, are you? That's right. Want your pillows plumped up, do you? I don't expect you want two, really: this one's all bunched up behind. Look – I'll take it away. Might as well sit on it myself if you don't want it. Nasty old hard chair, this is.'

She jerked the pillow from under Margaret's head, put it on her chair and subsided onto it, her thin legs crossed to expose a lot of thigh.

'Like my new dress, then?' She smoothed down her magenta skirt. 'I got it out of my catalogue, I'm an agent, you see, get quite a lot of orders, too.' she glanced at the flannelette nightgown which covered the shoulders of the woman in the bed. 'There's nightdresses and all in my catalogue: you should get Jean to order one from me, cheer you up a bit; all lace and that, ever so pretty. But still, you wouldn't get the wear out of it, I s'pose –' She left the sentence unfinished.

Vera came in with two cups of fresh tea.

'Here're the matches, Doris,' she said, throwing the box across the bed.

'Thanks,' Doris caught them and lit the cigarette in her mouth. 'I can't fancy a cup of tea without a fag.' She inhaled deeply and blew out a cloud of smoke, searching round her for an ashtray in which to put the spent match.

'Use one of those old saucers,' Vera suggested, pointing to the dresser.

Doris got up and eased a saucer out from behind its matching cup.

'Oops!' she shrieked, as the carefully-balanced cup teetered on its shelf. 'That was nearly a gonner! Proper old fashioned stuff, this is,' she said, examining the bone china with its delicate flower pattern. 'My Gran used to have stuff like this. I gave it away to the jumble when she died, glad to get rid of it. Can't understand Margaret hanging onto it: like something a bit brighter, I do, but it wouldn't do for us all to be the same, would it? I expect Jean'll make a few changes, anyway, when –' She nodded and winked, indicating the silent figure in the bed.

She perched on her pillowed chair again, cup in one hand, cigarette in the other.

'Connie'll be here soon, I expect. I left the door open for her.' Smoke from her cigarette hung in a blue swirl round her and Margaret coughed weakly.

'Coughing now,' Vera said, eyeing the sick woman critically. 'Don't like the sound of that. A good dose of that new stuff, Coffoff, would soon stop it. I'll tell Jean when she comes back.'

The two women sat sipping their tea and eyeing each other.

'I like your dress,' Vera said. Cheap rubbish, she privately thought, and a nasty colour, flashy; but then, what could you expect? She was glad she'd put on her lilac; elegant, it was, and suitable for the occasion, sort of half-mourning. 'I like a quieter colour myself, but it's very striking.'

'Cooee! Yoohoo!' a voice shouted from the kitchen, making Margaret wince. 'Anybody in?'

'That'll be Connie,' Doris said. 'In here, Connie!' she shouted back.

A large woman panted in, hung about with shopping bags and plastic carriers.

'Them shops!' she gasped. 'Talk about crowded! Buses is just the same, too; packed! But it's always the same sale-time, isn't it?' She descended hugely onto the chair Vera had pulled out for her. 'Got some bargains, though; wait till I show you! Is that a cup of tea?' She peered at Doris through the smoke haze. 'Get us one, Vera, do! I'm parched. Hello, Maggie!' she shrieked, belatedly noticing Margaret's pale face on its one pillow. 'All right then, dear?'

The women talked, mostly all at once, shouting each other down on their recollections of the fatalities due to taking green pills, looking at Margaret from time to time to compare her condition with that of their various relatives just prior to their decease, scandalously gossiping about their neighbours and screaming with laughter at the more slanderous of Doris's comments.

Connie, her thirst assuaged by two cups of tea, displayed the bargains she had just acquired with much delving into capacious bags and rattling of carriers.

'Phew! There's some fug in here,' she complained. 'Turn the gas down a bit, Vera.'

Without pausing in her description of the much superior bargains she had bought in the sales Vera leant down to the gas tap. The flames heating the perforated white pipeclay above them shrank and popped.

'Not right down,' Connie directed, and, still without pausing in her peroration, Vera turned the tap a half turn back. The flames flickered very low.

'That's right,' Connie approved. 'Any more tea going, girls?'

Vera jumped to her patent leather shod feet and bustled into the kitchen, returning in a few minutes carrying a tray.

'No sense to keep running in and out,' she said. 'Thought I'd bring it in to save time. I've put an extra cup on for Peggy: I saw her out of the window and she'll be in directly. Haven't seen Peggy for ages, not since the church social – and talking of that,' she sat down and leant forward conspiritorially, the tea forgotten for a moment, 'before she gets here I must tell you what I heard –'

Margaret coughed.

'All right, dear?' Vera asked automatically, scarcely glancing at her. 'Well, *they say*,' she began, her eyes bright with malice, '*they say* that Peggy –'

There was the sound of a door shutting and footsteps on the kitchen lino. The women leant back in their chairs quickly, giving each other winks and knowing glances, shuffling their feet and clearing their throats.

'Hello, everyone; it's me,' a voice called. 'The door was open so I came in, like you said.'

'Hello, Peggy!' the women chorused.

'Come in, love; pull up a chair and have a cuppa,' Vera invited warmly. 'We was just saying – wasn't we, girls? – we was just saying we hadn't seen you since the church social.'

Peggy waved her hands in front of her face.

'I say, you've got some fug in here, haven't you? Can't see across the room, hardly.' Connie had begged a cigarette from Doris and they were both puffing away. 'Like the black hole of Calcutta, it is. Mind if I open the window a crack?'

She edged between the seated women and the pushed-back table to get to the window.

'No, don't open that side!' screamed Vera. 'I don't want to sit in a draught!'

Peggy obligingly opened the other half of the casement so that the cold air blew across the bed.

'That's better,' she said, sitting down and accepting her tea cup. 'I can't stand a fug. How are you, then, Margaret?' she shouted. 'Enjoying a bit of company, are you? I always say a bit of company cheers a person up when they're feeling poorly.'

Margaret felt dreadful. Her head swam and throbbed with the noise: a cold wind blew across her face from the open window but did little to dispel the smell of smoke which caught at her throat – or *was* it smoke? Doris and Connie had finished their cigarettes but a pervasive smell hung heavy on the air. She raised a hand weakly from the folded sheet, trying to attract attention, but nobody noticed.

It was like being in a monstrous hen-house, the sick woman thought; cackle, cackle, cackle. Jean had been so careful to keep the house quiet for her these last few weeks; Jonathan and the older children had been so sweet and considerate – and now this. It was too much, and she felt a helpless sob rising in her throat, but suddenly, when she knew she could bear the noise and smell no longer, it seemed to fade, to become remote from her. Her breathing, which had become laboured, eased; she felt almost comfortable, drifting on a different plane, somehow apart from the clattering, chattering women.

*

Margaret had known them all their lives, these women sitting shrieking round her bed; had liked none of them much and had had her doubts about them, too. In an inexplicable way those doubts were doubts no longer: she *knew*.

Vera, sitting there smugly talking about Hilda as though

she'd been fond of her when in fact she'd loathed and resented her. Poor old Hilda; she was a gentle creature, never did anyone a bad turn in her life. A spinster, she'd been, and had a lot of money left her by her father when he died: being the only one in the family with no-one to fend for her he'd left her all he had; not a lot by some standards, perhaps, but a fair bit, nevertheless.

Sister-in-law Vera had taken Hilda in: kind, people had thought that was. Kind? That money she'd been left had infuriated Vera; unfair, she thought it was; should have come to Wilfred, her husband, and if she was baulked of getting her hands on it through him she'd try another way. She'd taken Hilda into her home all right, but she'd half starved the poor old soul, treated her abominably, made her do all the house work and taken every penny off her that she could; charged her rent, made her pay the rates and the TV licence – not that she was ever allowed to look at it – *and* saw to it that she made a will in her favour.

What a fuss she'd made when Hilda died, weeping crocodile tears; she was still making a fuss about it, always on about it being the doctor's fault, those green pills – how stupid, they were mild painkillers – but Margaret *knew* whose fault it had been, or rather whose *plan*, that she should die. No warmth, no comfort, no kindness, practically nothing to eat, the poor old thing had no chance, no desire to survive.

As for Hilda's brother, Wilfred, *he* hadn't noticed what his wife was up to, far too busy carrying on with that thin-legged, henna-haired, flashy Doris, her with her coarse ways. A magnet, she was, for a certain type of man, the weak, hen-pecked sort of man Wilfred was. Margaret couldn't count the men Doris had led astray, but she could see some of them in her suddenly-lucid mind's eye: the milkman, the baker's roundsman, the man from the Co-op, the man who came to read the electricity meter and most of her neighbours' husbands – Wilfred, of course – and who were these? – Connie's husband, and Peggy's.

That Connie, too, sitting there among her purchases. Purchases? Very few of them had been bought. Most of the stuff strewn round her had been filched, shoplifted, stuffed into her capacious shopping bags in the crowded confusion of the sales. She'd been doing it for years, Margaret suddenly knew; lift anything, she would, whoever it belonged to, and look at her now, showing off her stolen goods to Peggy.

Peggy: what had Vera been about to say just as Peggy came in? But Margaret knew. It seemed that, unaccountably, she knew everything, and Vera had got it wrong – or at least only half right. It was inevitable that rumours should have started to get around, and it was these rumours that Vera had been about to impart to the others – but it was much worse than she had heard, very much worse. Poor Peggy. But she must warn Jean –

Jean? Dear Jean! She could see her daughter's life spread out in front of her, from the moment she was born till now, like an animated map. She had got into scrapes as a child – what child hadn't? – some her mother hadn't known about, was seeing for the first time now, but nothing bad. She had married, perhaps not as well as her mother might have wished for her, but well enough, and she had been happy; the odd quarrel with her husband, the odd tired day when the children had been unjustly smacked were the exception, not the rule.

Perhaps Jean's heart had sunk at the thought of taking her widowed mother into her home? Margaret's anxiety was only momentary. No; Jean hadn't felt she *had* to take her mother in, she had *wanted* to, and had genuinely enjoyed having her. Thank heaven for that! She would hate to die thinking she had been a burden.

Would hate to die? Why had she thought that? Was that what she was doing, dying? Well, she'd known it wouldn't be long and it was really very interesting, this sudden facility she had acquired, this ability to see everything so clearly, to understand things she had never understood before.

For a moment she brought her orbiting mind back to here and now with an effort. Noise: cold: that strange smell. It would have been nice to stay until Jean came home, but she couldn't wait another moment, she was going, going. Her body felt strangely and pleasantly light, as though she were floating into a blissful sleep.

*

Jonathan tugged at her mother's arm as the bus drew up.

'Mummy, look! A fire engine!'

Jean followed her son off the bus, handing him the parcel containing his smart new blazer and cap, and looked where he pointed.

The glittering red vehicle stood at the end of the road at the bottom of which the bus had stopped. There was an ambulance beside it and a police car was parked nearby.

'My God!' she gasped. 'It's outside our house!'

There was not much left of the house. Most of the roof had gone and the end wall was a mass of rubble. The end wall was the dining room wall.

'Mother!' Jean screamed, and started to run.

The firemen had put out the blaze and ambulance men were climbing about on the rubble. The police sergeant tried to comfort the sobbing Jean.

'Your mother was almost certainly dead before the explosion,' he said, as an ambulance man put a blanket round her shaking shoulders and his companions slid the last of the stretchers into the white van.

'She was dead, love, honest,' the youngest one said. 'The explosion blew her clear and there wasn't a mark on her: she was lying as peaceful as though she'd just fallen asleep. You can see her, if you like.'

'Oh, Mum, Mum!' she sobbed, as the ambulance man pulled back the corner of the blanket to reveal Margaret's serenely smiling face.

'But the explosion –' Jean asked dazedly some minutes later. 'What explosion?'

'We shan't know for certain, not until we've made a complete investigation,' the police sergeant said, 'but it seems likely that a low gas flame was blown out by a draught from the window, and then one of the women lit a cigarette –'

'*One* of the women –?' Jean was too shocked, too confused, to make sense of what he was saying.

*

Margaret continued to float effortlessly, seeming to rise above everything, no longer hampered by her ailing body or distressed by the noise of those tedious women; but suddenly the all-enveloping peace was shattered by a loud bang. For a startled moment she wondered what it was, then realised that it was no longer any concern of hers – but what was this other noise? Voices, dreadfully familiar voices, not far behind her.

'I always said you smoked too much, Doris!' screamed Vera, who had never said any such thing. 'If you hadn't lit the match this would never have happened!'

'Oh, wouldn't it?' Doris screamed back. 'And who turned the gas down so low, then?'

'I only did it because Connie wanted it turned down –' Vera began, swiftly reapportioning blame.

'It would have been all right if that fool Peggy hadn't opened the window!' Connie was not about to be made the scapegoat.

'You thieving old hag!' Peggy rounded on the fat woman: recent events, however shattering, were forgotten as light dawned on an aspect of her erstwhile friend's character about which she had had her doubts but had never been sure of before. 'You didn't *buy* those things you got in the sales, you *stole* them, just like you've been stealing things off my washing line for years –!'

'And mine!' Doris chimed in. 'And what about my purse going missing that time? *You* had it, you bitch!'

'Don't you go naming names, you strumpet!' Connie shrieked. 'You've been thieving more than purses, you have! Pinch anybody's husband, wouldn't you? I know about you and my Bert; you and your flashy clothes –'

'You devil, Doris! You were after my Wilfred, too!' Vera chimed in, her worst fears of what her husband did all the time he said he was working on his allotment suddenly fully realised. 'You've been carrying on with just about every man in the district, you dirty little slut!' she screeched.

'Shut up, you murderous old cow,' Doris snarled. 'What about your Hilda, then? What about Hilda, eh girls? Green pills you said was the reason she died, but we know different! You made that poor woman's life a misery –'

'You killed her!' Peggy cut in shrilly. 'You starved her and made her leave you all her money!'

'You!' Vera turned on Peggy in outraged fury. '*You* dare to criticise *me* after what you did –?'

The women's shrieks merged into a cacophony of pure

venom as they all turned to castigate Peggy. With new-found and effortless speed Margaret fled away from their caterwauling towards a sort of misty radiance ahead of her. The filmy clouds parted slightly and she could see someone standing there, someone vaguely familiar. It was Hilda.

Hilda looked happy and – not younger exactly, but refreshed in some way; renewed.

'Hello, Margaret,' she said chattily, as though they'd met in the street. 'Well, this is nice! But what brings you up here? Vera said it was the green pills that did for me; over and over she said it, but it wasn't. I was too frightened of her, and too stupid, to even guess what she was doing to me then, but I'm not any more.' She peered over Margaret's shoulder. 'Talk of the devil – here she comes now! I've got a few things to say to her!'

'You'll have to wait until you can get a word in edgeways,' Margaret said wryly. 'The others have just found out what she did to you, too, *and* what they've been doing to each other, but they're all going for Peggy at the moment.'

'Poor Peggy,' Hilda said compassionately. 'She must have been very unhappy to have behaved like she did.'

'It'll be a long time before they feel they've punished each other enough,' Margaret went on. 'It'll take the best part of eternity, I should think.'

'Oh, look!' Hilda exclaimed, still craning her neck to see into the misty distance. 'They're not coming this way after all! They seem to be going down!'

The women's voices were becoming fainter, if no less acrimonious.

'Well, that's a mercy,' Margaret said, looking down at the steadily descending figures. 'Poor things; I bet they're giving each other hell.'

XII

The Whisperer

John Marsh

1

The Royal Infirmary,
Bradford.
November 24th 1909

Dear Robby,

I would value your advice. At the moment I have a patient who was brought in as a casualty. Evidently he had been visiting the Parsonage at Haworth. He slipped and fell down some stairs while coming from the upper rooms. He suffered severe concussion.

He appears to be well on the mend and is almost ready to be discharged. But he is obsessed with the idea that he has been 'taken over' by the spirit of Branwell Brontë! He claims that Branwell possessed his body when he was unconscious, and that when he falls asleep Branwell talks to him!

I know of your keen interest in all things to do with the famous literary family, which is my reason for writing to you. Mr Clayton does not warrant much attention from our top people here. After all, there is little wrong with him but a knock on the head without any complications.

So I get most of his ramblings which mostly concern his talking to Branwell Brontë when he falls asleep. I would not take much notice ordinarily but as every dream is apparently about Branwell the whole thing seems odd and I thought it would interest you.

I don't suppose you will have any suggestions but I felt I should ask.

All the best,
    Yours,
        Alec

'White Gates'
Raymond Road,
Keighley.
November 27th 1909

Dear Alec,

I was interested in your letter. It is a popular talking point among Brontë students that the Parsonage at Haworth is haunted, though little of this has reached the general public.

Yet there are several stories told of a shadowy figure – a man's – being seen about the Parsonage. More than one visitor has spoken of sudden changes of temperature before the apparition – if such it be – is seen. This spectral figure is usually observed leaving the room where Branwell died.

Of course, one can discount this as vivid imagination on the part of people who perhaps are influenced by the dismal atmosphere of the Brontë home which, even on a sunny summer's day, is a gloomy enough place in all conscience.

I would very much like to talk to your Mr Clayton. I'd like to weigh him up and make up my own mind as to whether one can believe what he says or if he is making it all up for some purpose of his own. To gain sympathy?

    Yours,
        Robby

The Royal Infirmary
Bradford.
November 29th 1909

Dear Robby,

Your letter arrived the day Mr Clayton was discharged from my care. I gather that he was returning immediately to London. He was passed as fit and well and there was no point in him staying on here any longer.

I spoke to him before he left and he still insisted that when he falls asleep he talks to Branwell Brontë. I hope that when he resumes his everyday pursuits – I gather that he holds a fairly important position in the City of London – that he will recognise his obsession for what it is: a dream state that will end as he regains his full health and spirits. I wonder what Sigmund Freud would have thought of all this!

Do come and have a meal some time next week. Clara was saying only yesterday we hadn't seen much of you and Martha lately. She will drop Martha a note and fix something for next week. I looked forward to seeing you and tell you more about the mysterious Mr Clayton.

In haste,
Yours,
Alec

2

No one will believe me but this is how it came about. I, Edmund Clayton, went to Haworth to see the Parsonage. I had heard so much about it, had read everything the famous sisters had written, as well as every book about the family. I had even read Branwell's poems and his part completed novel.

It was not until November that I had a chance to leave London and travel north. I had some holiday due – I am my father's partner in the family wine and spirit business in the City – and I had forgone my summer holiday because of pressure of work.

My friends thought I was mad going to Yorkshire when I could have gone to the Riviera or somewhere further afield like Egypt.

But as I sat in the train one bright November morning, I felt I was setting out on some strange adventure and that, at the end of the journey, something would be waiting for me, something I could not possibly guess at.

I took a cab from Keighley, the nearest town to Haworth, and took a room at the Black Bull Inn hard by the church and the famous Parsonage. It was afternoon and after I had had a late meal, I made my way, with the church on my left, to the old house at the end of the lane beyond which were the wild moors so beloved of the young Brontës sixty years ago.

Because it was November with scudding rain clouds replacing the bright sunshine and blue skies of the morning, there were few people about in the village.

I rang the bell and was admitted to the house by the custodian, a bent old man, and soon was going from room to room examining the many Brontë relics in their glass cases.

I saw the sofa on which Emily had died, the portraits on the walls, the bookcases, the writing desks the sisters had used. I went up the stone staircase and gazed into the bedrooms, got a glimpse of the moors from a back window.

Rain was falling. The short afternoon was closing in and the rooms were dark and chilly. Two other people, who had been looking over the house before me, left. I heard the front door close behind them.

The footsteps of the custodian died away as he returned to his quarters at the back of the house. Had he forgotten me? I wondered.

I went into the front bedroom and looked across the graveyard to the church looming against the dark sky. There in their tombs were all the Brontës save poor Anne lying in her lonely grave in a Scarborough churchyard.

Did I imagine a light touch on my shoulder? I turned but there was no one there.

I shivered. It was a cold dank house, yet in the last few minutes it had seemed to grow even colder. Suddenly I wanted to leave it and go back to the warm bar parlour of the Black Bull Inn.

I came to the top of the stairs. The custodian must have heard me moving about for his voice came up to me.

'It's time to close, sir!' he called.

'I'm ready to go!' I called back. 'It's a dismal place on a November afternoon.'

I looked over my shoulder. It seemed to me as I peered into the shadows behind that something moved. I thought I heard a whisper:

'Don't go! It's so lonely, so very lonely!'

'But I must go! I don't belong here!' My voice sounded strange. I hardly recognised it as my own.

The shadow seemed to move towards me. I panicked and took a step forward. Too late, I realised I had misjudged my position on the landing. Where I had expected firm flooring under my feet before the stairs began there was nothing.

I stumbled, tried to regain my balance then pitched

forward. I missed the step and had a curious sensation of floating; then something hit me a violent blow on the head and I knew no more ...

When I came to I was in bed. Someone was talking in a low voice near at hand. I tried to see who it was but screens round the bed hid them from me.

'Where am I?' I called and one of the screens was pulled aside.

A woman in nurse's uniform came into the cubicle. She smiled down at me, a kind gentle smile.

'You're in hospital,' she said quietly. 'You fell.'

'Fell! I don't remember.'

'Try to get some sleep,' she urged, smoothing the coverlet. 'You'll feel better when you wake.'

Obediently I closed my eyes. Almost immediately I was dreaming. Or so it seemed.

I was in total darkness. Someone was whispering.

'Who is it? Who is there?' I asked.

My voice sounded strange in my ears, strained, high pitched.

'It is I – Branwell,' the whisperer said. The words were clearer now. 'You and I are now one. Thanks to you I have escaped from that damned Parsonage.'

'Branwell – Branwell Brontë!' I cried. 'How can you be he? He's been dead for many years.'

'That is my misfortune.' A note of satisfaction filled the voice which now seemed to be inside my head. 'Now I have a chance to escape. For you are to help me.'

'How can I do that?' I demanded.

'By dying, my friend. When you die, I die, too. Then at last I will be free.'

The voice ceased. I called out. But there was no answer.

I woke suddenly. The doctor was by my side. He was a cheerful young fellow, the medical registrar; as such he had introduced himself earlier.

'You're a lucky man, Mr Clayton,' he said brightly. 'You might have fractured your skull in such a fall, for you hit the wall at the bend of those stairs pretty violently. However, the X-rays show that you've sustained nothing more serious than concussion. You should be up and about in no time.'

In one way I felt relief. In another I was worried.

Had I been dreaming about Branwell Brontë? It had all seemed so real in the dream. For of course it had all been a dream, nothing else.

'Doctor,' I began hesitantly, 'do you think it's possible when one lies unconscious and consequently helpless that one's body might be entered by – by the spirit of someone who – who's been dead for a long time?'

I felt a fool talking like this but somehow I couldn't help myself. I had to be reassured by someone and who better than a doctor?

The young man burst out laughing.

'Well, that's a strange thing to ask,' he cried. 'Are you suggesting it happened to you?'

I frowned. I felt annoyed. Why should he laugh at me? I was quite serious.

'Yes, I am suggesting it happened to me,' I said, a trifle sulkily.

'And who do you think has taken you over?' he chuckled.

I turned my head away. If this was the best he could do I'd drop the subject.

He must have seen he'd upset me. He must have realised too that a sick man must be humoured.

'Tell me a little more,' he said quietly. 'I'm sorry I laughed. You took me by surprise, that's all.'

So I told him of my experience in the Haworth Parsonage, the feeling that I had not been alone on that upper floor.

'I would never have pitched down those stairs left to myself,' I said. 'I have good sight and hearing and there was light enough to see by.'

'You believe you were pushed?'

'I do!'

'But you were the only one upstairs! The custodian was below. All this was brought out by the constable who went into the house after your fall.'

I felt tired. I did not feel like arguing with someone who obviously thought the knock I had had must have upset my mental processes temporarily.

'You get some sleep,' the doctor said. 'I'll look in and have another chat with you later.'

He did. By that time I had slept again.

'Any more dreams?' he asked in the jocular tone he probably used to all his patients.

I had. As soon as I had fallen asleep the whispering had started again. At first it was a babble of sound. I picked out little more than a few isolated words.

Die. It's so easy. Try. Please!

Then the voice steadied.

'You will help me to escape, won't you, sir?' There was a despairing sob in the voice now. 'Please! You are my only hope.'

The voice faded then ceased altogether. I wakened to find the doctor at my bedside. He had a dressing gown over his pyjamas. His hair was tousled. He had obviously been called from his bed.

'They told me your temperature was up and that you were very restless,' he said. 'What is it – another dream?'

I nodded. He looked impatient. His voice held more than a hint of irritation when he spoke.

'Mr Clayton, your dreams are brought on by the concussion you have suffered from your fall,' he said. 'Because your accident happened at Haworth Parsonage you are allowing your imagination to run away with you. Certainly you *will* dream about the Brontës. At present you are obsessed by them. But in a few days you will be back to normal. Once you return to London and your day-to-day life the events of the past couple of days will fade and cease to trouble you.'

Perhaps he was right, I thought. Pray God he was!

'You must be patient, Mr Clayton,' he said, then checking a yawn. 'I hope I find you much improved in the morning.'

A few hours later he was at my bedside again.

'Any more dreams?' he asked, an infuriating twinkle in his grey eyes.

I nodded. 'Branwell spoke to me as he does whenever I fall asleep. He wants me to commit suicide.'

His eyes widened.

'But why should he want you to do that?' he asked.

I could see he was humouring me again. I stared coldly back at him.

'How long will it be before I am fit to leave this place? I

would like to return to London,' I said.

'I'll give you another examination this morning,' he said. 'I don't think we shall keep you much longer. There's very little wrong with you, you know.'

I did not comment on this. Not much wrong with me! How would he like it, I wondered, if another man had taken lodging in his body?

3

The Royal Hotel
Paddington
London.
December 18th 1909

Dear Alec,

It was good of you to give me Mr Clayton's London address when we came to dinner with you and Clara last week. I know you were reluctant to do this bearing in mind medical ethics and similar scruples you felt at the time.

I am glad you gave in to my persuasive ways. I feel I must write to you and let you know what occurred when I called on your ex-patient last night.

He lives with his parents in a pleasant house in Bayswater near Kensington Gardens, which accounts for my present address. It is only a short walk from this hotel to 54, Lancaster Way.

I called round yesterday afternoon and Mr Clayton's mother told me that her son would be returning from the City for his evening meal at six o'clock. She said she would say I had called and would tell him I was returning at half-past eight.

Accordingly I had my own dinner and, at the appointed time, walked through the grey foggy Bayswater streets to Lancaster way. A maid servant answered the door and said that Mr Edmund was waiting for me in his study and she would take me there. I did not see the older people, for which I was thankful.

Mr Clayton received me with a rather puzzled stare. I could see that he could not understand why I had called to see him. I imagine he had suspicions that I was a salesman of some sort.

I quickly reassured him and stated my business, which was to enquire if he had fully regained his health. I told him that as I was in London you, dear Alec, had asked me to look him up and enquire if the progress shown under your care had been maintained.

He assured me that it had though as he spoke I noticed a certain secretiveness in his manner as if there was a great deal he might have said but that he had no intention of confiding in a stranger.

You will want to know about his appearance. You are aware, of course, that he is a tall good-looking man of perhaps thirty, fair-haired, blue-eyed, well-dressed and with the confidence of a successful businessman. Yet apart from this there was something about his looks and manner that puzzled me. It was as if his outward appearance was a veneer, as if beneath the surface of smiles and friendly words there was something else. It was as if, as he chatted light-heartedly about his experience in Haworth and at Bradford, he was thinking of something else. It may sound ridiculous but he gave me the impression that while he was talking to me he was talking to someone else at the same time. The latter conversation did not need words. Clayton certainly did not utter any.

He offered me a drink and gave me a very good malt. I complimented him on it and he said it came from a friend of his in Edinburgh. The conversation flagged a little and I realised I had better show my hand – or go.

'Mr Clayton,' I said, 'Dr Conway told me a little about the time you were in his care. I was intensely interested in what you had told him for I have been, for many years, a student of the Brontë family. I especially took notice of what he said about your experience at the Haworth Parsonage and later in hospital.'

He glared at me. At first I thought he was going to order me from the house as an inquisitive busy-body, for he stood up and loomed over me in quite a threatening manner. Then suddenly he shrugged and turned away. He finished his whisky and poured another.

'What exactly do you know?' he demanded, turning back to me. The firelight glowed in his eyes which seemed to have receded beneath his heavy eyebrows. The fire, too, seemed to have added red tints to his fair hair.

'I know only what the doctor told me,' I said rather uncomfortably. 'I understood him to say that you dreamed about Branwell Brontë when you fell asleep.'

He sank into the armchair facing me across the hearth and stared into the flames.

'It still goes on,' he said in a low voice. 'Sometimes I dare not sleep, at others I long for sleep as a man dying of thirst longs for water.'

'What form do these dreams take?' I asked gently.

He stared at me in anguish.

'They are not dreams, Mr Haines,' he muttered. 'They are very real experiences though I don't expect anyone else to believe me.'

'Would you be prepared to tell me more, Mr Clayton? I will reserve judgement as to whether or not I believe you until I have heard you out.'

He jumped up and insisted on pouring me another generous dram; then he returned to the hearth and stood staring down into the glowing embers, his back turned to me.

'I think that your friend, Dr Conway, did not take me at all seriously,' he said. 'He thought that as I had had a nasty knock on the head, and because my experience was associated with the Parsonage at Haworth, I should naturally dream about the Brontës. I made one or two attempts to convince him that it was more than that but he insisted that, when I resumed my normal life I would regain my old health and spirits.'

He gave a hard bitter laugh.

'Regain my old self! By God, if only I could!'

'You are upsetting yourself,' I said. 'I think I had better go.'

He swung round on me with an angry shake of his head.

'No, stay!' he cried. 'I must talk to someone and you are a stranger. It might be easier talking to you than to someone closer, a member of my family, an intimate friend. You see, Mr Haines' – he was standing over me now – 'when I fall asleep Branwell Brontë possesses my body. He tells me what I must do when I wake. It is very simple. He says I must kill myself so that he will escape from this life to the next.'

I said nothing to this. What could I say? The man was in a terrible state. Better to hear him out. If I could help him I would. If not at least he would feel better by unburdening himself to a sympathetic listener.

He began to pace up and down the room.

'All this must seem completely ridiculous to you, Mr Haines,' he said. 'I'm a reasonably intelligent person. I hold an executive position in the family firm. I live a quiet life and enjoy several interests of a not very exciting kind: reading, theatre going, eating out with friends. In fact until I took that accursed journey to Yorkshire I thought of myself as an ordinary sort of person with the tastes and interests of most bachelors of my age and upbringing.'

He stood staring before him. His lips moved but no sound issued from them. He seemed to be talking to someone though no one was visible.

At last he looked back at me. He seemed almost surprised to find me still there.

'Your dreams?' I prompted. 'What of your dreams since you returned to London?'

He drained his glass and put it down on a side table.

'My dreams!' He laughed but there was no humour in the sound. 'You call them dreams. My interlocutor has a different view, I feel. It is more a conversation than a dream. It has one theme and one theme only. I am urged to commit suicide.'

I bit my lip. I longed to help him. He needed someone trained in pyschiatry to help him.

'You need advice,' I said quietly. 'Perhaps a doctor who understands the mind –'

He bared his teeth. His eyes flashed.

'How can you say such a thing?' he demanded. 'What medical man could help me? How do you treat someone who has had his soul taken over by another? No, Mr Haines, there is no treatment for a case like mine. I must go on – to the end.'

I felt very unhappy. What could I say to him? It was a problem which only time could solve. Perhaps later the dreams would cease and he would regain his normal mental health and spirits.

I rose to go.

'You must forgive me for staying so long,' I said, and when

he did not speak or make any effort to restrain me: 'May I tell Dr Conway a little of what you have told me?'

He shrugged. 'If it gives you any satisfaction you may. But he will only laugh.'

'I don't think he will. He may pity you but he will not laugh. Of that I am sure.'

I held out my hand and he gripped it fiercely. His face was within inches of mine. I could feel his breath hot on my cheek.

'Mr Haines, you have listened to me with real sympathy and I am grateful.'

He hesitated. I waited. Had he something else to disclose?

'There is one other thing,' he muttered looking into my eyes.

What else could there be? I wondered. Surely he had told me everything.

'Yes?' I asked encouragingly when he did not speak.

He shook his head violently. His lips moved though no sound came. He turned his head and seemed to look at someone – or something – in the corner of the lamp-lit room.

Suddenly he faced me again and burst out with:

'He does not wish me to tell you. But I mean to!' His voice was shrill. 'Until three nights ago he spoke to me only when I was asleep. But now – now he talks to me during the day, at home, in the street, in my office. Now he urges me to obey him – night and day.'

I looked round. I wondered if I might see a dim figure crouching in the corner. But there was nothing.

Clayton unclasped my hand.

'Go now,' he said and there was a great weariness in his voice. 'I have told you everything.'

'I would visit you again,' I said unhappily, 'but I must be with my family at Christmas. But do take care, and try to regard this matter as of passing importance. In the New Year I will come again. I will hope to find you much improved in mind and body.'

He did not seem to hear me. He turned away and stared at the wall at the back of the room.

I let myself out and made for the front door. No one saw me leave the house and make my way through the foggy streets back to my hotel.

I will be in touch with you, dear Alec, shortly after I return to Yorkshire.

With all seasonal good wishes to you and Clara,
    Your friend,
        Robby.

                      'White Gates'
                      Raymond Road
                      Keighley.
                  January 15th 1910

Dear Mr Clayton,

I am sorry I did not manage a trip to London as I told you before Christmas might be possible. Business commitments have kept me in Yorkshire though I hope to travel south fairly soon.

I am still very interested in all you told me when I called to see you in December. Perhaps you might feel inclined to allow me to entertain you to dinner one evening?

Hoping to hear from you at your convenience.
    Yours sincerely,
        Robert Haines

                      'White Gates'
                      Raymond Road
                      Keighley.
                  January 23rd 1910

Dear Mr Clayton,

I hope to visit London on Monday next. Will you join me for dinner at the Royal Hotel, Paddington, at 8 p.m. and we can have a long talk?

I trust all goes well with you as I did not receive a reply to my last letter.
    Yours in haste,
        Robert Haines

                    54, Lancaster Way
                      London. W.2.
                  January 24th 1910

Dear Sir,

I am replying to your letter of yesterday's date addressed to my son, Edmund Clayton.

I am sorry to inform you that my son died in a drowning tragedy four days ago. The interment took place in the Paddington Cemetery yesterday afternoon.

May I hope that, if you come to London as you mention in your letter, you will call to see me?

Yours faithfully,
Hector Clayton

The Royal Hotel
Paddington
London. W.2.
January 28th 1910

Dear Alec,

As I told you when I saw you in Bradford last week I intended to call on Edmund Clayton when I visited London a few days later. Before I left I heard from his father that his son had died in a drowning tragedy and would I go to see him.

Accordingly I visited 54, Lancaster Way this evening and, because I know you are interested in this unhappy affair, I am writing to tell you what transpired at my meeting with the senior Mr Clayton.

He received me courteously. He is a man in his sixties, a tall pleasant person obviously very upset at the tragedy which has robbed him of his eldest son. There is a younger son who has recently married and lives in Brighton. I did not see Mrs Clayton who is evidently prostrated with grief, and keeping to her room.

Mr Clayton told me that his son had died attempting to save the life of a child who had slipped and fallen into the Thames and was in danger of being swept away on the ebbing tide. Edmund Clayton had apparently been walking along the Embankment when he had heard shouts and, looking over the Embankment wall, saw the little boy struggling in the water. Apparently he had not hesitated but had jumped into the river and swum with the child to the nearest steps. There willing hands had pulled the child ashore. However, before Edmund Clayton could be saved he had, in his exhausted state, slipped under the surface and been swept away. His body was recovered on the following day far down river.

It was a fairly common tragedy, I suppose; but there are

one or two puzzling features. Mr Clayton said he had never before known his son leave the office early and walk along the Embankment. Certainly he was not likely to do so on a bitter winter afternoon. Also one of the rescuers had told his father that he felt he could have helped Edmund on to the steps after others had carried the child to safety. But he said that as he held his hand out for Edmund to grasp the young man had said something that sounded like 'Goodbye!' before he sank below the surface and disappeared.

Mr Clayton told me that he was proud that his son had shown such bravery in forfeiting his own life for that of a child, though it was desperately hard losing him.

'He gave his life for another,' he said, tears streaming down his cheeks.

As I walked back to my hotel later I wondered if, perhaps, Edmund Clayton had given his own life, not for one other but for two. Or am I being fanciful?

I hope to see you, Alec, when I return. Martha will be writing to Clara to ask you both to come to us for dinner.

    Yours,
        Robby

XIII

Mandrake

Kelvin I. Jones

> 'I do not find
> The Hanged Man.'
>
> – T.S. Eliot, *The Waste Land*

Harry Potter paused for a moment, then laid down the scythe. Pulling a handkerchief from his trouser pocket, he wiped his glasses, then dabbed at his forehead.

It was hot, so hot that the shirt he was wearing clung to his armpits, forming two round stains there. He glanced back at the cottage, wondering whether to go in and pour himself a long cold drink. His left hand was sore and swollen, where he had grasped the handle of the scythe.

He looked at his watch. 12.30. When he had begun at nine, the garden had lain in shadow, a wild overgrown place of enchantment which he had been reluctant to disturb. The old brick wall, well over six feet high, was broken only by a high oak gate, secured by a rusty padlock. Once inside, he had stood staring at the tangle of ivy, convolvulus and wild flowers with a childlike innocence that his friend Carter had found hard to understand.

It was Carter who had invited him here, all those months ago, Carter the retired civil servant, Carter the naturalist, Carter the Devonian by adoption. He had always taken the lead in their relationship, even when they were at public school together, so it came as no surprise when the phone rang on a dismal winter evening and Potter was offered the cottage as a place of rent-free retirement.

Potter had accepted at once. Although Carter and he had been lovers years ago, all that was in the past. Now their friendship was a platonic one. They shared an interest in many subjects: botany, water-colours, cookery. Honeysuckle Cottage was the ideal place to pursue such hobbies. Carter would live at Brook Farm half a mile away and, in return for his kindness, Potter would provide his friend with all the produce he could raise from the half acre around the cottage.

Which was why Potter was clearing the garden on a hot June afternoon. He tied his handkerchief around the handle of the scythe and got back on his haunches again.

The blade sheared through the undergrowth, briars and nettles falling in waves about him. There was a dank smell to the earth, an odour of long decay which rose into his nostrils. The soil was rich and black here. Through the nettles he could discern a rectangular hump. Its edge was so distinct it might well have been man-made, perhaps the remains of an old rockery. Yet there were no large stones to confirm this.

He kept the arm swinging, despite the pain in his left shoulder. The mound was clearly discernible now. There was a channel running around it, roughly six by four feet in dimensions. And there was something else, a splash of purple, half-concealed by the foliage.

Potter parted the weeds with the scythe. A cluster of thick, hairy leaves lay there. White and purple flowers sprang from their midst. It was like an ugly, misshapen orchid, the centre thrust out like a hideous ox's tongue. The sight of it made him reel. Then he was conscious of the smell again, a rank earthy odour, more powerful now, rising from the soil.

Hesitantly, he touched the leaves, then smelt his fingers. The stench was a powerful composite, of long-rotted vegetation and fungus. Once, years ago, he had split a decayed tree trunk and smelt the same. The memory had remained locked within him until this moment.

He continued to stare at it for several minutes, surprised that anything so luxuriant could ever grow here in this place of darkness, for the grass that stood high on either side was dense and the walled garden let in little light. The plant was unfamiliar to him but he was sure Carter would be able to identify it.

With great care he severed the nettles around his find, laid out his pocket handkerchief, then went to the garden shed and returned holding a trowel and a large flower pot.

Soft black soil shifted slowly from the base. The roots appeared to extend some way beneath the surface. Using the trowel to gain leverage, he pulled at the plant with his free hand, but it refused to budge. The smell was stronger than ever now, a dense acrid odour that made him feel nauseous.

Cursing, he cleared a wider area of soil from the visible root. Long and clefted like a hand, it extended far down, out of sight. Its texture was peculiar to his touch, like dead skin that had dried beneath the sun.

At last the root gave, and he fell backwards. There was a sound, something like a cry of pain. He stood up, looked about, but there was no one in the overgrown garden save himself.

The pot was too shallow for the plant's exceptionally long root. Deciding to postpone his grass clearing, he walked back to the house clutching his new find. Once, he looked back, conscious of someone watching him.

*

Inside, the house was relatively cool. He laid the plant on some sheets of newspaper and went upstairs to find a new shirt and trousers. There was a long vase under the kitchen sink which would be just the job. Taking off his jeans, he caught sight of his legs in the mirror. They were long and spindly and covered in black hair. Oddly, his legs resembled the root he had had such difficulty dislodging from the ground. The thought amused him.

The iced lemonade was very welcome. Harry passed his index finger along the line of reference books in the sitting room and pulled out an encyclopaedia of rare flowers and plants. None of the colour plates bore the least resemblance to the thing he had found in the garden. After ten minutes' browsing, he gave up and sat in the big basket chair. On the table roots stuck out like the feet of a corpse. It was an exceedingly ugly plant.

He examined the flowers. Their texture was curious, soft and membranous, like the tissue of an eyeball. He drew back his finger in disgust. Potter felt tired and oddly ill at ease. He laid his head back on the cushion of the sofa and closed his eyes. Soon he was sleeping.

*

He was lying in the walled garden. Above him, the sun beat down out of a cloudless sky. Nevertheless, he felt icy cold.

There was something unfamiliar about his surroundings. The garden differed from his memory of it. Many of the wild flowers were not the same and the walls of the garden looked newer. Wild herbs he could see, rosemary, saxifrage, thyme. Yet he could not distinguish their essence, for over all hung the unremitting stench he now recognised so well. He could taste it on his tongue, a thin layer of sourness.

He wanted to get up, but his limbs refused to obey him. He tried opening his mouth to say something but his teeth remained clamped as if someone had wired them together.

He looked about. He was stretched out on the humped rectangle of earth. He recognised its dark, granular soil, its damp shimmer.

There was an uncomfortable certainty within him, as if someone had placed him here. He was lying here, waiting, waiting for something to happen.

He closed his eyes, hoping the dream would be dispelled, wishing it would go away. But when he opened them again the garden was still there, the smell heavier than ever. The desire to wake up was strong within him now.

There was the sudden sharp sound of the wicket gate opening. He tried to turn his head but he could not. A rustle as of loose clothes against foliage approached, stopped, then grew closer. A shadow fell across him, a long, thin pointed shadow and, from somewhere close behind, came the steady rasp of stertorous breathing.

*

Potter woke up. The sun was blazing at him through the kitchen window. He stood up uncertainly, his legs still feeling their paralysis. So vivid had been the dream that he almost did not dare to open his mouth. But he overcame his fear, turned on the tap and saw the ice-cold water spiral into the beaker. A thought occurred to him and he picked up the telephone.

'John? Harry here. I've just found something I can't identify. Yes, in the garden, that's right ... might interest you, love ... Fine.'

John Carter's interest in botany was all-consuming. In five minutes he was at the front door, his round face beaming.

'Well?' asked Potter, after a decent interval had elapsed.

'You'll not believe this when I tell you.'

'Try me.'

'It's a mandrake.'

'A *what*?'

'A mandrake. Of course it's rare. Exceedingly rare.'

Potter poured out a cold beer while his friend filled in the details.

'It was very popular in the Middle Ages, particularly among alchemists and necromancers. Half man, half dragon, they called it. No doubt the peculiar root gave rise to that idea.'

'Why was it so popular?'

'It was used as an emetic, sometimes as an aphrodisiac.'

Potter raised his eyebrows. Carter grinned.

'Actually the leaves contain a narcotic substance. I've not tried it myself of course. You cut the root up or boil the leaves.'

Carter said that if Potter dropped by the following day he would lend him a book entitled *The Herbarium* which contained a reference to the plant.

They finished their drinks. Potter showed him the door.

*

By evening the lassitude that had descended on Potter earlier still had not diminished. He placed the plant in an ill-fitting vase, left it on the kitchen windowsill, then took a bath to ease his pains.

He had always made it his custom to read in the bath and tonight was no exception. Lying back amidst the steam and smell of bath oil, Potter flipped idly through the pages of the little local history book Carter had given him as a present to mark his arrival in the village.

At page 46, something caught his eye.

Gibbet Hill [the text ran] marked the intersection of the old coach road with Flower Street. In former times the crossroads here could clearly be seen, and in the 18th century they achieved some notoriety as a place where highwaymen and cattle thieves were hung up in chains. With the coming of the nineteenth century and the opening of the Exeter road, the coach road (and the crossroads) fell into disuse. Today there is little to be seen except stretches of footpath. Parts of Brewer Street (erected in the 1860's) were built over the road, the garden of Honeysuckle Cottage enclosing the crossroads itself ...

The text swam before his eyes. His brain strove to make a connection, but the heat of the bath and the vapour of the water overcame him. The book slipped from Potter's hands ...

He was dreaming again. This time he was not in the garden, but beneath a huge oak tree, waiting for something to happen. Absurdly, the book he had been reading was still within his grasp. On either side of him stood two tall men, both fair-haired, dressed in coarse smocks and leather aprons. Grim-faced and silent they were, prepared for some dire event.

A rattle of wheels sounded in the distance. Up the hill, led by an old nag, came an open cart, driven by an old man wearing a straw hat.

As the cart approached, Potter saw its standing occupant. The head was cowled, the face invisible, but he could discern the gnarled hands, knotted by rope.

The figure swayed, its black cloak flapping in the wind. Potter could make out a low, continuous sound coming from the figure, something like an incantation, though the words were not distinguishable.

The cart stopped. Leather Apron One approached it, unchained the side, then hauled out the cowled figure. From his belt, Leather Apron Two uncoiled a stout rope and, with slow deliberation, hurled one end of it over the bough of the tree.

Potter knew what was going to happen. He tried to turn away, but was unable. The force that rooted him to the spot emanated from the figure. Leather Apron One grabbed at his prisoner and a cloud of dust burst from the cloak. He stepped back, coughing. Leather Apron Two went to his assistance. Holding the noose in his right hand, he pulled at the man's hands. There was an oath uttered, then Leather Apron Two fell back emitting something between a gasp and a cry.

Potter stared disbelievingly. The hands had come away, sheared off in their entirety, leaving two sticks of bone ...

*

He awoke, but only just in time. The bath water was filling his nostrils, the soapy foam pouring into his mouth. He sat up, hands grasping the porcelain sides, gasping for breath.

There was a crash from somewhere downstairs. Intruders, he thought, in his confused state. Reaching for the bath towel, he stood up unsteadily and wrapped it around him. He could still taste the metallic sharpness of the bath oil.

The noise had come from the kitchen, but there was no sign of a break in, only a scattering of soil over the windowsill and draining board.

A sharp pain in his left foot made him step back, but it was too late. Blood oozed from a cut on his instep. Potter could see it clearly now, a web of glass shards spread out beneath the sink. The vase must have fallen and smashed. But that was odd, since he would have expected the glass to be spread over the draining board and sink. He investigated further and discovered the mandrake by the kitchen door. By their relative positions, he would have thought someone might have opened the kitchen window and hurled the vase across the room. But, the window had been locked.

Potter applied a plaster to his foot, swept up the soil and repotted the plant, though he did not tarry long, for the smell in the kitchen was beginning to overpower him.

Then he went to bed.

*

Saturday was even hotter. Harry cleared the remainder of the garden, put refuse into sacks, then walked to the village where he purchased a taller vase. He had been half afraid the plant would die, but it appeared unharmed by its ordeal.

On his way back, he dropped into Carter's home where he collected the book he had been promised. Potter told him of his discovery about the cottage, though he refrained from mentioning the dream.

'I knew about the old road of course, though I'd forgotten about the origin of the name,' Carter pontificated.

'You mean Gibbet Hill?'

'It was a common practice to bury suicides and devil-worshippers at crossroads – right up until the 17th century. You've heard about the Magus of Zenan, I suppose? He's mentioned in the book, I believe.'

Potter shook his head, picturing the soggy mess that was drying out on his windowsill.

'He was an Elizabethan court astrologer by occupation, though his more clandestine activities covered witchcraft and necromancy. It was for the latter that he was finally hanged.'

'Really? Where?'

'Here in Zenan, by order of the local justices. But surely you read the account?'

Potter stayed until teatime, then left for the cottage. Carter's authoritative manner had always jarred, but this afternoon it did not seem to worry him. He had other matters to think about.

*

The large, leather-bound volume had been marked at chapter 32. Potter opened the book and glanced down the page.

> This herb [it ran], which is called mandragoras, is powerful and efficacious. You must gather it in this way when you come to it: it shines like a lamp in the night. When you first see its head, then at once make an inscription on it lest it should escape from you. Its power is so great that it will immediately escape from an unclean man. Inscribe it with iron and dig up from the earth with an ivory staff. When you see its hands and feet, then tie it up. Of this herb it is said that it has so great a power that whatever thing pulls it up will soon be deceived in like manner. Therefore as soon as you see it jerked up and it is in your power, then at once

take it, twist it and wring the juice out of its leaves into a glass pitcher.

There followed a learned speculation as to the true nature of the mandrake. The author favoured the theory that the plant originated from the sperm of a hanged man. At this point, feeling somewhat disgusted, he put the book down and left the room.

*

Some while later he went back into the kitchen and stood by the open window, thinking.

It was absurd, of course, but it was something which continued to preoccupy him. If he tried it out on himself, just a small infusion, and the thing worked ...

His mind went back to Carter's friend, David. He had only met David once, in a gay bar in Exeter, but they had immediately struck up a rapport. Unlike Carter, David was tall and fair. Unlike Carter he was much younger, a bright, intelligent young man with a university background and a wide circle of friends of a similar disposition.

Potter realised how he resented Carter. His patronage, his overbearing manner were things which had helped to terminate their physical relationship years ago. He looked at himself in the mirror, saw the crows' feet and the frown lines, thought of the years of slow decay at Honeysuckle Cottage as Carter grew more immobile and increasingly dependent on his services. Then he pictured David, his sharp eyes, his bright laughter and olive complexion. He picked up the phone.

'David? Good, you're in. Harry here. Yes, John's friend ... Good, glad to hear it ... Listen, I was wondering if you were doing anything special tomorrow night?'

Potter smiled.

'How would you like to come round for a meal? No, at the cottage. No ... just us ... Sure ... Good ... About 8 o'clock tomorow night? That'll be great ... see you!'

Beaming, he put down the receiver, then drew a large vegetable knife from the kitchen drawer. It was a shameful thing to do, of course, but he would try it out on himself and if there were any ill-effects, well ...

The concoction was bitter, a disgusting, earthy taste which made his breath smell. He gulped down the contents of the glass, then rinsed out his mouth thoroughly. As far as he was aware there were no side effects, just a slight feeling of drowsiness. He decided he would retire early.

*

It was dark when he awoke. The room was stifling and oppressive. He turned to the bedside table and switched on the lamp. Then he paused to listen. There it was again, that same rustle he had heard in his sleep, a sound as of paper dragged along the ground. It was almost inaudible, yet he was sure he was not mistaken. He crept downstairs, foolishly aware of his nakedness, a walking stick held in his clenched fist. Methodically he checked each room. Everything lay undisturbed. Except, that is, for the kitchen. It had been clumsy of him to leave the window ajar. The vase had been close to the edge and the plant must have toppled into the sink again. The sound of the vase smashing had awoken him. He picked up the broken pieces and disposed of them in the bin. However, he could find no trace of the mandrake.

It was puzzling. Feeling tired and oddly depressed, he returned to bed, where he lay awake thinking of David. It had been foolish of him to believe what Carter had said about aphrodisiacs. He felt slightly ashamed at what he had done.

*

The darkness smothered him like a blanket. Closing his eyes, he edged his way into sleep.

He was lying in the garden. In his left hand he clutched an empty cup. He was conscious of awaking from a profound sleep where images danced and flickered against the darkness. Faces were there, lean cheeked pallid faces, eyes that burned with a cold fury, mouths that leered at him. His conscious mind tried to push back these ghosts but they remained, imprinted on his retinae, gesticulating at him, murmuring his name.

He raised himself up. The sun beat down on him, parching his lips and in his ears was a persistent buzzing. He looked about.

The garden glistened in the sunshine. At first, he thought that it was the height of summer, for the plants bore a sheen the like of which he had never seen. They were unfamiliar plants, with exotic bell-shaped flowers and furry tendrils. Plants with vivid green leaves that curled like rows of tongues in his direction ...

A sound broke his reverie. He looked up, his vision blurred. He heard the wicket gate creak on its hinges, then he realised that he was looking at David.

David smiled at him, a lazy knowing smile which Potter thought he understood. He saw that David was naked to the waist, his long fair hair falling onto his shoulders. Beads of perspiration ran down his arms and chest. David kneeled down to speak to him.

'I have been busy, Harry, busy in the garden, busy preparing a place ...'

Harry nodded, thinking of the high wall and soft undergrowth, looking at David's olive skin and broad shoulders.

'David,' he replied, 'I'm so very glad you're here. Let me get you something to drink.'

He tried to get up, but his legs resisted him. In the silence that fell between them, he noticed that there was no bird song, only the sound of insects seething in a vast tapestry against the garden walls.

David smiled at him. His left hand, the hand he had all the while been holding behind his back, now revealed itself. It held a scythe, a long, sharp-edged scythe whose blade glinted in the sun.

Harry's eyes moved from the scythe to David's hand. The hand was not what it should have been. The skin was not smooth and the nails were not manicured like David's. The hand was old and dry, brittle as ancient parchment. Through the cracked skin Harry could see white bones protruding.

David raised his arm, the arm with the gleaming scythe, the arm where the bones and sinews cracked like dead firewood. Harry screamed.

*

When he awoke, Harry was still screaming, but this time it

was not because of the dream. At first he thought that the buzzing inside his head was but the awful memory of the garden. He imagined that the sheets were damp with perspiration, that the soreness at the base of his neck was from where he had ricked it in sleep. But when he placed a hand there and felt the rough, scaly texture, and the thing moved, if ever so slightly, he tried to push it away, then realised he was too weak to move.

He stared at the bed linen, unable to comprehend. Everywhere, over sheets, blankets and pillows, the dark red stain of his life-blood spread.

He turned his eyes, gasping for breath. Overpowering, the smell smothered him, its acridity shutting off his oxygen. He had smelt it in the dream, smelt it when David had walked into the garden, yet he had chosen to ignore it, to deny its summons.

Feebly, he attempted to raise his other hand to his throat. He caught a glimpse of the black root there, chafed and pared where he had severed it with the vegetable knife. But now the root was whole again. One small bead of blood shone through the punctured skin.

His vision blurred as the mandrake settled itself and he felt the last of his strength ebbing away. Through half-closed eyes, on the other side of the bedroom, he saw the hood of a cowled figure, heard its breath rasp in anticipation.

His hand fell onto the bloody sheet ...

*

It was some while before David recovered from the shock of his visit. On entering the house by the rear door, the first thing he noticed was an overpowering smell which he found so tangible he was forced to step back for a moment. When Harry did not respond to his calls, he wandered from room to room where he noticed (to his alarm) a large number of blood spots and traces of garden soil.

He did not dwell on what awaited him in Potter's bedroom, though the police pressed him on that point. One matter which he kept returning to was the paleness of Potter's body which, David said, 'seemed as if it had every last drop of blood drained from it'.

The coroner's verdict was one of suicide, though, as John Carter pointed out in his statement to the police, Potter neither suffered from depression nor had he ever mentioned taking his own life.

Not long afterwards, John Carter offered Honeysuckle Cottage to David as a rent-free domicile and, since lodgings near the University of Exeter were always exorbitantly expensive, David jumped at the chance. Since Potter's death, his relationship with the older man had strengthened and grown more initimate. Carter liked the idea of someone on whom he could try out new ideas, while David thought it a small price to pay for the occasional evening of comparative tedium. Besides, he found Carter physically quite undemanding.

There was, however, one condition to which Carter insisted that David should adhere. That was the maintenance and well-being of the garden. David, being naturally athletic, was only too glad to comply, especially since his terms of tenancy stipulated this.

So it was that he discovered the mandrake. Of course, he did not know what it was, nor did he bother to inform his friend Carter. It lay on a rectangular piece of black soil, roughly six feet by four. David thought how fresh and loose the earth looked, as if it had been newly turned over.

At first, he did not wish to disturb the plant. It shimmered and blossomed in the July sunshine, its leaves glossier than ever, curled like tongues. David felt a reluctance to cut it down, but then he remembered that he had better keep his side of the bargain.

David raised the scythe.

Somewhere, from one of the tall trees that overlooked the garden, a bird stopped its song.

XIV

Swing High, Willie Brodie

Fred Urquhart

I

While I watched the fire spread through the Theatre Royal's auditorium I thought of young beautiful Sarah Siddons in the arms of tall, dashing Macheath. I thought, too, of the day I was hanged. I think of that day often. That day had been such a great disappointment to me. Such a surprise after all my careful planning to cheat not only the hangman but the crowd of smug civic worthies of Edinburgh, all dressed in their braws, who had come to gape at the ceremony on the platform outside the Tolbooth prison.

Well to the forefront of the city's magistrates was my fellow town councillor Geordie Fairfax, a man I could never abide: a big brosy-faced chiel with a stomach as big as the backside of a drayhorse. Fairfax's house had been one of those I'd burgled after I'd dined at his table and seen the lie of the land. I was never able to stand the way Fairfax was forever indulging in bawdy talk, even inside the council chambers, always sniggering and encouraging folk to snigger with him. I liked him even less now as he leered at me, rubbing his hands together and shouting: 'Swing high, Willie Brodie.' I tossed my head, ignoring him and the rest of the roistering keelies come to see my degradation, and I swaggered onto the scaffold ahead of my snivelling accomplice Smith. They'd all laugh on the other side of their faces when news came later from abroad that Deacon William Brodie was still alive and fairing well. I had the steel collar hidden under my kerchief, and the hangman had been extravagantly bribed to put my halter on a short rope.

Geordie Fairfax shouted again: 'So ye're still struttin' like a turkey cock, are ye, Willie Brodie? This is the last time ye'll strut, ye wee turd.'

I fain would have thumbed my nose at him, but it was beneath my dignity. I stuck out my tongue instead, and it was still sticking out when I came to my senses standing in the long queue at St Peter's Gate. I couldn't speak; I was choking with more than rage at the hangman's double-dealing and the uselessness of the steel collar. I was still choking when yon half-blind saint shook his head, and two brazen young imps of Satan cheekily prodded their fiery forks into me and urged me along the lower path to the nether regions. Though I must grant that they did unloose my tongue and stopped the choking, and so I was able to thank them. One imp said: 'You are welcome, sir. I hope you enjoyed being swung. It was a most noble exit.'

'There is nothing noble about getting hangit,' I said. 'Nothing noble about death, if it comes to that. And of course we must all come to it sometime. But I think there's been some mistake. I was intended to have many more years yet.'

'I fear your plans miscarried, dear sir,' the other imp said. 'Your friends have already collected your body and are now conveying it in its coffin to the cemetery near George's Square.'

'That ill-gettit hangman,' I said. 'I was full certain he'd been paid enough, but seemingly not. I trust I'll be able to pay him in other coin in time.'

'That I prophesy you will, sir deacon,' one imp said. 'Do not take it to heart. Rest assured that you will become a legend in Edinburgh and spread alarm among its citizens for centuries to come. You will have the last laugh, sir ghost.'

I remembered this as the flames grew higher and higher and a burst of cold east wind sent them skittering towards the Royal's roof. Was I having the last laugh by destroying something I loved? For I have always loved the theatre and its players, particularly my divine Mrs Siddons.

II

I was hanged in the year 1788, on the first day of October. I was forty-seven years of age, and I congratulate myself that I looked younger. So you might say that I was hale and hearty when I started my stretch in limbo. I worked hard at learning the tricks of the ghostly trade, and it wasn't long before I got my ticket-of-leave and was free to go and haunt wherever I pleased. I went straight to Edinburgh.

First I attended to the hangman for double-crossing me. I gave him as big a surprise as he gave me. I burgled his house and threw all his ill-gotten gains in the North Loch. Then, after he'd eaten a hearty breakfast, I followed him to the Tolbooth where he was to hang a couple of young lads for sheep-stealing. When the lads were brought onto the platform where I'd stood myself, the hangman was quick to put the ropes around their necks, but Willie Brodie was quicker. I pushed one lad aside, put an invisible noose round the hangman's neck, and before he knew what was happening I'd given him the fatal drop. I was waiting for him with his tongue sticking out when he reached the other side. 'Ay there, my good man,' I greeted him. 'Do ye recognize me? I hope you got as big a shock as I did. And now if it pleases you I'll have my money back.'

I attended next to Geordie Fairfax and terrorised him for a good few years until a day came when he could take it no longer and I had the satisfaction of witnessing his passing with eyes and mouth wide open, his hands clutching his throat. Even now in this hereafter, where all are supposed to be equal, I often manage to play a trick on him and make him shriek with pain. The Geordie Fairfax of yesteryear has vanished, and there has never been a snigger nor a bawdy word out of him ever since.

And then it was the turn of the sanctimonious Edinburgh worthies who had turned up their long nebs with disdain when my double life was laid bare. I always rub my bony hands with satisfaction at the way I have revenged myself on them and their children and their children's children. I have haunted them in divers ways, but mainly I have haunted them by flames. Every mortal is feared of the spreading flames of a fire that has got out of control. And almost every mortal is feared of the fires of Hell that await him, terrified he will burn amidst them for eternity. And nobody fears hell fires more than the men and women who have set themselves up to be holier than God, always pointing fingers of scorn at those they consider beneath them, their forked and fiery tongues always spitting venom at the raffish, the lowly and the unfortunate. There were many such folk in Edinburgh. I had been well aware of them ever since I was a bairn. I had observed them closely. For one of them was my father, Francis Brodie.

My father was a rich and highly respected cabinet-maker, who had been elected Deacon or head of the guild of Edinburgh cabinet-makers. His father had been a Writer to the Signet, so Francis was brought up in the shadow of the law. He married my mother, the daughter of another lawyer, in 1740. I was the first of their eleven children. Following family custom, my father saw that I was well educated. Then when the time came he insisted I follow his footsteps and become a cabinet-maker. I rebelled. I was ambitious to go to sea as a midshipman and become an admiral. My father would not listen to my pleas to become a seafarer. A cabinet-maker I was to be. I gave in with an ill grace, applied myself diligently to my trade, and became an even better cabinet-maker than my father, creating many beautiful tables, chairs, desks and chests and other fine pieces to decorate the homes of the gentry. And after my father died I became the Deacon of the cabinet-makers guild like him, was equally well respected, and I was the friend of many of the wealthy and was invited regularly to their homes to be a guest at their dinner parties.

As the years passed I hankered no longer to be a sailor. By that time my imagination was in the grip of two other great passions – gambling and going to the playhouse. Some evenings I went to the cockpits in the shadow of the Grassmarket and wagered for high stakes with shady characters. Other evenings I was taken in my sedan chair to the Theatre Royal in Shakespeare Square, and I sat in my box and applauded the actors that pleased me. My favourite play was Mr Gay's *The Beggar's Opera*, and I've lost count of the times I have been delighted and ensnared by Mr West Digges's performance as Macheath the highwayman. I admired Mr Digges profoundly. He was a big handsome fellow and walked with a swagger that I envied. I envied more than his swagger. I envied his height. Since the time I was a lad in my early teens I have wanted to be much taller than my five feet, four inches. I have always disliked, too, my sallow complexion and the scar on my left cheek. My large brown eyes I am used to, and I have nothing against them. But I'd fain have been better looking and stood at least two inches over six feet.

I blame my father for my lack of inches. Indeed I blame my father for what the complacent and the self-righteous call my path to perdition. If my father had not thwarted my ambition I doubt if I'd have carried out the robberies that became the talk of Edinburgh, the night-time breaking into houses with the help of George Smith and the two other callants that the Justices called the Brodie Gang.

Since I was hanged I've laughed often at the sight of my father's face when I met him once in the nether regions. I was prepared to let bygones be bygones and was approaching him with open arms when he cried out: 'Begone! Begone, you scoundrel! How dare you bring the noble name of Brodie down in the dust! You are no son of mine but a spawn of old Beelzebub. Get back to the depths where you belong. Begone into the flames!'

My father's words gave me the idea for the fires that I have started in numberless houses and public buildings in Auld Reekie ever since. Some of the fires never came to anything, for the officious had doused the flames before they could get a good hold. But some of my fires have been of noble dimensions and have caused tremendous damage. Each has given me great satisfaction at the panic I have created in the hearts of the smug, the censorious and the intolerant.

The first of my huge fires was the one that destroyed so many of the old pends and wynds and closes of Edinburgh's Royal Mile in the year 1824. The fire raged for three days; hundreds of folk were made homeless; and the gentry were feared that the fierce gale would blow the flames down to their new houses in Princes Street and beyond. The Tron Kirk and St Giles Cathedral were set alight, but the firefighters managed to save them. By the time the fire was out most of Deacon Brodie's Edinburgh had vanished forever, and it delights me to record that the Tolbooth, where I'd spent so many weeks chained by a leg to an iron bar, was burned to the ground.

It was in the Tolbooth that I yearned first for the young and beautiful Sarah Siddons. I heard from the turnkey that she'd come to act in the Theatre Royal. She was to appear in two or three plays and was to give a special performance as Lady Macbeth. I'd had the pleasure in the midst of vast misery and anxiety of seeing Mrs Siddons act as the ambitious and bloodthirsty Scottish queen that time in London when I was trying to escape abroad. While waiting for a ship I appeased my impatience by visiting the playhouse in Drury Lane and saw Mr David Garrick in one of his better-known parts and, as well as Lady Macbeth, I had the joy of watching Mrs Siddons as Queen Catherine pitting her powers against those of her brother John Kemble as King Henry VIII. It was the last joy I can remember in my earthly life; I went to Holland afterwards to wait for a ship to the city that once was called New Amsterdam. I never saw it. The sheriff's officers from Edinburgh caught up on me hiding in a cupboard in old Amsterdam, and I was extradited and brought back to the Tolbooth.

So, when I heard that my favourite actress was appearing on the stage less than half a mile away, I begged the turnkey to let me out for an evening to see her again. I promised with my hand on my heart that I'd come straight back to my cell and the chain that clamped so fiercely to my leg. The turnkey laughed and sent for the ironmonger, a fellow who'd worked once for me but had been sacked for bad workmanship, and ordered him to strengthen the links on the leg-chain.

'Aw, did I hurt ye then, Maister Brodie?' said the fellow, leering as he gave my leg a bang. 'My hammer slipped, I'm that excited at meetin' ye again. Such a great pleasure to see that ye're still hale and hearty. Though it'll not be for long, Maister Brodie. Aw no, the days are gone when ye held the whiphand ower yer workers. It's a great pity ye can't gang to the theatre to see yon painted lady. But never mind, ye'll soon be the leading actor on a stage yersel'. I'm looking forward to seeing ye perform on the gallows. I'm having the last laugh on ye, sir, so maybe that's what's making my hand so shaky!'

On the Tolbooth's site there is now a heart composed of

stones set in the ground – the Heart of Midlothian – a heart that is a memorial to the hearts of all those unfortunates housed and tortured in the dismal old prison. It could be my heart. For many years it has been a custom for people visiting the city to stop in the High Street and spit on this heart for luck. What luck can they expect from expectorating on the anguish and fates of countless lost souls? I'd fain like to spit in the faces of all tourists who spit on the heart of William Brodie. And so the fires are for them as well as for the self-righteous.

III

I have, as yon imp of Satan prophesied, become a legend in my native city, but not because of the fires. These fires have never been laid at my door, except by the imaginative. They are a secret between me and Auld Nick and the half-blind Saint at the Gate. They are something I keep up my ghostly sleeve, a card that will trump everyone else's at the Judgement Day. It will be my last trump.

My legend was created first by friends who spread the tale that I had, after all, cheated the hangman, and that the coffin in the George's Square cemetery was empty. Many were foolish enough to believe this, and they looked fearfully for me in the dark wynds and courts, expecting to be knocked down and robbed. But the greatest contribution to the legend of Willie Brodie was that of another Edinburgh birkie, Robert Louis Stevenson, a sickly young man who was quick to leave the city and go abroad to become an author of renown.

When I met Mr Stevenson soon after he died on an island in the Pacific a hundred and six years after I died so cruelly myself, we agreed that neither of us could abide Edinburgh's eternal East wind with its blustery showers. Nor could we abide the cold-blooded, snobbish and puritanical gentry that turned up their wind-and-whisky-reddened nebs at everything they considered lewd and vulgar. Most of all, however, we agreed that there was nothing we loathed more than the dreary ding-ding-dinging of kirk bells that filled the Scottish air from dawn until dusk every Sabbath.

Mr Stevenson told me he'd put the memory of the bitter Scots puritan frost into the essays in his volume *Picturesque Edinburgh*.

'And a lot of our fellow-countrymen have never forgiven me for it,' he said. 'A great many Scots think nobody's as clever as they are, so they're jealous of anybody who proves to be cleverer. They don't like writers, and they go out of their way to damage them, even when they have no cause. They're wonderfully vindictive haters up there in the North.'

'I know that, man,' I said. 'I know it to my cost.'

'Mind you, Mr Brodie,' he said. 'It was mostly your own fault that you came a cropper. You tried to be too clever. You wanted to be Macheath. You wanted to be tall and dashing like him, so you turned thief to frighten people and tower over them. You believed that if you imitated Macheath you'd become him, and so this led to your execution.'

'That is probably true,' I said. 'And I ken another thing that's true, man. Mrs Peachum is correct when she says: "All men are thiefs in life." It is not only money and property and valuables that we all steal.'

'I daresay,' Mr Stevenson said. 'Every man wants to get more out of life than he brings into it, and it saddens him not to take it away when he departs.'

'I ken that only too well,' I said. 'But knowledge does not lessen many of my problems.'

'Does one still have problems in the hereafter?' Mr Stevenson said. 'I thought I'd got rid of mine when I presented myself at the Gate and St Peter said: "Pass, friend, you do not need to give the countersign." '

'And what are your problems, sir?' I said.

'I am not sure yet who I am,' he said. 'All my life I have had three or four people inside me, all struggling to get out and declare themselves on paper. Sometimes I've had ten or eleven fighting each other in the same book. I had hoped that in this other world I'd have got rid of them. When you were a laddie, Mr Brodie, did other children call ugly names after you?'

'Not that I can recall,' I said. 'If they had I'd not have been long in giving them a severe clout.'

'I was always afflicted in that way when I was little,' R.L.S. said. 'Other bairns often ran after me shouting, "Half a laddie, half a lassie, half a yellayite." '

'What did they mean?' I said.

'A yellayite is what we Scots call a yellowhammer,' he said.

'But maybe they did not call the bird that in your time.'

'Ay, they did,' I said. 'I ken what a yellayite is. But what I don't ken is why these bairns could think you were divided into three. I ken now that I'm divided into two, but I can't see myself divided into three. Especially not as a yellayite. Though maybe death's bright glare has made my sallow complexion even yellower?'

'Don't haver, Mr Brodie,' R.L.S. said, laughing. 'I was only wondering if you'd had the same troubles as I had.'

He then informed me that he and a friend, a poet fellow called Henley, had written a play about me; also that I'd been the inspiration for one of his greatest stories *Dr Jekyll and Mr Hyde*. He was going to tell me about this story when an angel called and whisked him away to a higher astral plane to meet another important author. I have never seen R.L.S. since, though I have searched for him often.

What Mr Stevenson told me intrigued me mightily. Although I seldom read when I was alive – always being too occupied in doing other and more profitable things – I had a great desire to read this book and see what I appeared like in print. And so I searched for a copy in the houses in the New Town, in the grand homes of the gentry in Queen Street and Abercrombie Place. And it was in Heriot Row, where Mr Stevenson himself was born, that I found it at last. Though not in the former Stevenson home but five or six houses away. *Dr Jekyll and Mr Hyde* was being read in bed every night by a pretty young lady who was a slow reader. I was a randy lad, and I'm still a randy ghost, so I had difficulty in controlling my passions as I leant over this bonnie lass and read word for word with her as she turned the pages. I did not want to scare the young lady by laying a ghostly claw on her. Deacon Brodie has no wish to frighten bonnie lassies; it's their parents and grandparents that are my prey. So I confined my attentions to the book, and what I read dumbfounded me. I wanted to ask Mr Stevenson what he meant by such slander but, as I've said, I have never seen him again.

IV

We ghostly spirits live on many different astral planes, yet you might think that we would fraternise, that we'd meet often for couthy cracks about the horrors we've given to this body or that. That is not the case. There are many well-kent ghosts I have never met, although I've been in the nether world now for two hundred years.

It was long after she died, for instance, that I met up with Mrs Sarah Siddons. One day in 1831 I heard on the grapevine that she was dead, so I went to London to hover over her funeral. But her ghost had two days' start on me, and I'd missed her in transit. I returned in haste to the other world, but nobody knew to which astral plane she had gone. I searched and searched, but it was useless. And as I searched my love for her grew to grand proportions until I could think of nothing else but having her in my arms.

It was 1897 before I met up with her, however. I did this with the help of a fellow Scot, a poet called Thomas Campbell who wrote those memorable poems 'Lord Ullin's Daughter', 'Hohenlinden' and 'The Battle of the Baltic'. He also wrote a life of Mrs Sarah Siddons, and that is how we became acquainted.

Mr Campbell told me that the great actor Sir Henry Irving was to unveil a statue of Mrs Siddons at Paddington Green in London. Her ghost would attend the ceremony, and Mr Campbell would accompany her as one of her oldest friends. And so it came about that I also attended this ceremony and Mr Campbell introduced me to the lady who had for so long been the darling of my heart.

We started off on a somewhat bad footing. Mrs Siddons' ghost, who looked now as the lady had chosen to look at the peak of her career, that is aged about forty, turned on me like a viper. 'So this is the theatre incendiary who has been pursuing me for over half a century!' she cried. 'I have no wish to know the destroyer of so many theatres.'

'I have burned only one theatre, madam,' I said, bowing. 'The Theatre Royal in Edinburgh. That is not the old Theatre Royal in Shakespeare Square. I left that theatre alone because

I did not wish to harass its licensee, your daughter-in-law, Mrs Henry Siddons. But I had no qualms about destroying the other Edinburgh playhouse, the Adelphi. I burned it down in 1853. It was rebuilt and called the Victoria. Then in 1859 when the old Theatre Royal was closed down, the Victoria changed its name to the Royal. I was so incensed at this that I burned it down again in 1863. It was rebuilt. I burned it down again in 1875. It was rebuilt again, and again I destroyed it in 1884. It was rebuilt yet once more, but in a different place, and so far I have left it alone. But one of these days the flames will engulf it again.'

'You are an enemy of the profession, sir,' Mrs Siddons said. 'I have no wish to continue our brief acquaintanceship. Come, Mr Campbell, let us get as far from this vandal as possible.'

'A moment, madam!' I cried. 'Just grant me one more moment of your celestial time.'

'Celestial? La la, what a romancer the man is,' she said.

'Naturally, I'm a romantic, madam,' I said. 'Otherwise I would not be a lover of the playhouse and its loveliest of players. I do not hate the theatre. If I did I'd have destroyed the old Royal long before Mrs Henry Siddons appeared there. But I revered the old Royal because you'd trodden its boards at the time I was in durance vile.'

'The man talks like an actor,' she cried. 'Proceed, Sir Rogue.'

'I never contemplated any damage to the old Royal,' I said. 'I'd loved it since I was a lad, and some of my happiest earthly moments were spent there. But when the new theatre adopted the name of Royal I was angered, and as I already had a vendetta against the town councillors who had authorised its building, my anger was intensified. I became full of spleen and started the flames. Yet I wept as I watched the blaze. I was like a child who has deliberately broken his favourite toy in order to draw attention to himself.'

'If you felt like that, sir, why did you burn the place again after it was rebuilt?'

'I do not know, madam.' I spread out my hands and looked upwards. 'Perhaps it was my revenge against those long-ago magistrates who condemned me so mercilessly. Perhaps it was a desire to vaunt myself. I do not know. Though I know I have no regrets for what I did. I am an incendiary. It gives me great pleasure. And, therefore, I shall continue to be an incendiary.'

'So the present Theatre Royal is not safe?' the divine lady said. 'You intend to set it alight too?'

'Never,' I said, laying my hand on my heart. 'Never as long as it gives me the entertainment it now gives. The playhouse has changed its venue. It is now situated at the top of Broughton Street. At the corner where Leith Walk begins, overlooking the area called Greenside.'

'I have not been in Edinburgh since my death,' she said. 'I do not know Broughton Street.'

'It is part of the city's development,' I said. 'Edinburgh has widened its horizons in many directions.'

'How interesting,' Mrs Siddons said. 'I must visit the place again sometime. But meantime I shall bid you goodbye, sir. Come, Mr Campbell, attend me back to whence we came.'

'Ay, we must all depart,' I said. 'I shall accompany you, madam. Now that we've met I have no intention of letting you out of my sight. I hope to take you very soon to Edinburgh so that we can view the new Theatre Royal together. It now gives a form of entertainment that should interest you. It is now called the Home of Varieties.'

'And pray, sir, what are varieties?'

'They are single acts or "turns",' I said. 'Turns composed of an actor or an actress reciting a comic monologue or dancing or singing. Quite often the performer does all of these. These acts are not what you, madam, were used to in your great days, but they are much appreciated by the plebeians who fill the pit and the gallery. The plebeians love what they call the "patter".'

Mrs Siddons said: 'How common.'

'Common or not,' I said. 'I derive great enjoyment from some of these turns. They are very amusing and make me laugh. Sometimes the tears run down my cheeks with laughter.'

'But then you are a common little man,' the divine Sarah said. 'Come, Mr Campbell, your arm.'

A rebuff like this means nothing to William Brodie. I pursued her like a hound after a fox, and in the long run I brought her to ground. She became my mistress. We loved and bickered and loved and scratched each other's skulls for decade after decade. And during these decades there were two world-wide wars and millions were killed, and new and larger astral planes had to be formed to accommodate all the new spirits. There were so many newcomers that the old ghosts became inclined to cling together for reassurance and, therefore, I managed to keep company with Mrs Siddons. In 1946 our little group decided to celebrate the end of the Second Great War by going to Edinburgh, almost the only city that showed no bomb-damage, and staging a production of *The Beggar's Opera* in the Theatre Royal. This was entirely my idea. I proposed it because I intended to be the producer and to act the chief role of Macheath opposite my divine Sarah Siddons as Polly Peachum.

Scarcely had we arrived in Edinburgh than we encountered a hitch. This was the ghost of Sir Henry Irving, who was already in possession of the Theatre Royal. Sir Henry had heard that Edinburgh proposed to hold a yearly Festival of International Drama, Music and Literature, and so he intended to stage a production of his great earthly success *The Bells*.

'I would have preferred to appear in the Royal Lyceum where Miss Terry and I had so many triumphs,' he said. 'But there will be so much human activity in the Lyceum and that other theatre, the King's, that it would upset my equilibrium.'

'There is no danger of that ever happening, Sir Henry,' Thomas Campbell said. 'However, you do not need to worry for a year yet. You have been misinformed about the date of the first Edinburgh Festival. It is not until 1947.'

Sir Henry was furious and said he'd sack his press agent. But he refused to budge from the Theatre Royal. 'First come, first served,' he said. 'To quote the lower classes.' There was an uproar at this, and Mrs Siddons and Sir Henry and I all screamed at each other, Thomas Campbell adding spice to the stir by caustic remarks. In the long run, though, we came to an agreement. Sir Henry would produce *The Beggar's Opera* and Mrs Siddons and I would play the leads. That seemed to settle matters, then Mrs Siddons used her new women's lib rights to play a fresh card. 'I will take the role of Mrs Peachum,' she announced. 'I am too long in the tooth now to play Polly.'

'Nonsense, madam,' I assured her. 'You will never be too old to play Polly.'

'I have more experience of the stage than you have, Sir Rogue,' she said. 'I know my limitations. And that, sir, is something you do not know. It is absurd for you to attempt the role of Macheath. You are too small.'

I gnashed my teeth with fury at the insult and cried: 'What do you mean, madam?'

'I mean,' she said, 'that you're not big enough for me. I like big men. Tall men. Tall men like the real Macheath.'

'There is no real Macheath,' I shouted. 'It is only playacting.'

'And I have had enough playacting with you, Sir Rogue,' she said. 'I shall appear in this production only if Sir Henry agrees to play the role of Macheath. You, sir, can shuffle away back to the lower depths where you belong.'

Perhaps our little tiff might have ended there, had we been alone, and we would have had the sweet reconciliation my soul desired, had not Sir Henry thrust himself dramatically between us and intoned in his best Lyceum elocution:

'Do as the lady asks, you little knock-kneed knave. You are the laughingstock of the underworld with your heroic postures and your endless prating about the so-called evils of your native city. I know Edinburgh as well as you do, Mr Brodie, and I have never seen any of these evils. I love Edinburgh. I came here to Mr Wyndham's theatre when I was nineteen and played over four hundred parts on its stage. I will never forget how Edinburgh audiences took me to their hearts. Begone, you low criminal, back to the lowest depths!'

The night of Irving's production of *The Beggar's Opera* brought ghosts from all parts of the astral planes for its performance. So many ghosts that if they had been in their earthly bodies it would have taken six or seven theatres to hold them. From my hiding place in the ticket-collector's cubbyhole at the gallery entrance in Little King Street I watched them congregate. At midnight the play began. I watched most of the first act and was lost in admiration for Mrs Siddons acting as Mrs Peachum. Then, at the interval, I stole beneath the stage and lit the pile of papers and other rubbish I'd placed there.

The rest is history. The Theatre Royal was completely gutted. The newspapers reported the blaze in detail, but never once was there any hint that Deacon Brodie had caused it. Nor was there any hint that the blaze had lost him the love of Sarah Siddons and that she had disappeared into limbo with Sir Henry Irving.

V

The Royal was never rebuilt. Its empty shell stood there for many years to remind passers-by of the great days of Tommy Lorne, Will Fyffe, Dave Willis, Tom Cable and other entertainers who had made them laugh. Then the empty shell was knocked down, and on part of its ground was built an enlargement of St Mary's Cathedral next door: the sacred taking over the profane. The rest of the ground was made into a car park. I have haunted this car park ever since. The netherworld now is too full for my taste of ill-tongued, bad mannered spirits; I would rather put up with the voices of my native city. So I return to the netherworld only occasionally to have my ticket-of-leave renewed. Old Pete always stamps it with great vigour and the last time he did it he remarked to one of the Recording Angels: 'Good riddance to bad rubbish.'

On the other side of St Mary's Cathedral there is now a public house called 'The Conan Doyle'. This name was meaningless to me until a few months ago. It was then that another ghost came to haunt the car park. We bid each other a civil time of night, but that was all. I resented his presence, and I sensed he resented mine. After a fortnight, however, we introduced ourselves. He is another native of Edinburgh, Sir Arthur Conan Doyle, who studied to be a doctor at the University and spent the rest of his life in England. He became a writer and created Sherlock Holmes, a character so famous that folk still go to Baker Street in London to gape at the house he was supposed to live in. Sir Arthur, who was interested in the occult long before he died in 1930 and saw the reality for himself, has usually haunted Sussex, where he lived in old age, still looking for a solution to the mystery of the Piltdown Man; but too many tourists in Sussex have driven him back to Edinburgh and when he found a tavern called after him he decided he'd stay. 'I'm so glad they didn't call it Sherlock Holmes,' he said. 'Do you know, Mr Brodie, nine out of ten know the name Sherlock Holmes, yet how many remember the name Arthur Conan Doyle? One perhaps in a thousand. So it is bliss to be remembered by my own name even if it's only as the sign of a public house.'

'I have not even that, Sir Arthur,' I said. 'Do you think that perhaps one day there will be a tavern called The Deacon Brodie?'

We talk about this often when we are thrusting our ghostly visages into those of people getting into their cars because Sir Arthur wants to show them there is an occult world that may perhaps be a better world than theirs. I am glad to say we have caused quite a few accidents.

Last night Sir Arthur brought me the news that a German birkie called Bertold Brecht, who wrote a play *The Threepenny Opera* based on Mr Gay's masterpiece, is to produce it at the next Edinburgh Festival. It is to be staged in The Playhouse, a theatre that used to be a cinema in Leith Walk, not far from the old Royal. Sir Henry Irving is to play the part of the head gaoler, a handsome young film actor who died young is to play Macheath (now called Mack the Knife) and Mrs Siddons, who has had her face lifted two or three times, is to be the heroine. I think that another Edinburgh theatre will go up in flames next year.

XV

The Nine Lessons and Carols

Lanyon Jones

I suppose you like ghost stories ... a silly question really, considering you've asked me to tell you one.

A ghost story for Christmas night ... well ... we have the traditional setting, with oil lamp burning by the wing armchair, the yule log smouldering in the ancient grate. I must admit the jazz you've got playing on the record player is not entirely conducive – but everyone to his own way, I suppose ...

Well now, a ghost story to tingle the nerves before bed. Not much, just comfortably enough. Far removed enough to cause the sensation of fright but not the real thing; mild amusement, but not alarm. No – that sort of thing would never do for this comfortable season, would it ... or would it?

Actually the story I'm going to relate occurred at this time of year. It was on the Sunday after Christmas, so I'm told, which occurred that year on December 30th. Yes, yes I'm almost certain that's what it was.

Well ... you gather that it's a true story; but being so it doesn't quite conform to the parameters we set for such things, does it? For it is not distanced by many years ... and is no vague half speculation because it was told me by a friend to whom it actually happened.

Oh yes – that's a problem too. It does not necessarily leave one feeling comfortably satisfied. Perhaps it's not quite the right thing for Christmas.

Well, if you insist. I suppose you can be the judge. But it will be too late then, won't it?

Oh very well ... It was, as I have said, told me by a friend to whom it happened, let us call him Stevas. And it wasn't some remote corner of England either; in fact we both know the place.

Stevas was staying with me. He had recently retired from being organist and choirmaster of this certain place. It was an ancient and very beautiful abbey, now the parish church of the small town that surrounded it.

Well, the story. We were walking back from midnight Mass at the cathedral. I remember the choir had been particularly good, with a quite exquisite treble solo, the first verse of 'Once in Royal David's City'. He mentioned the choir, saying how surprised he was that the boys were allowed to stay up so late. I told him that the matron of the choir school had sent them to bed at eight o'clock and got them up again at ten-thirty, so they didn't miss much sleep. But didn't the choir at – (we haven't called it a name, have we?) sing at midnight, I asked, for they were very famous. I remember his sharp reaction, his sidelong glance as we were coming down the path to the deanery. I could see his face clearly for it was a bright starlit night. It wore a sudden wariness, as if I were probing, trespassing ...

'No!' he said, very adamantly. 'No, they're not allowed to sing in the abbey late at night.'

It was the reaction that intrigued me, and once indoors, a late night drink in his hand. I prevailed upon him.

I think it must have been that it was Christmas Eve, or rather Christmas morning, that moved him to tell me the story. It must have been preying on his mind. Perhaps he even wanted to make some kind of confession ... But anyway he told me the story as it happened to him and that is, word for word, what I am about to relate to you, and it's true, to that I can swear, because I got it from a friend.

The thing began after he had only recently been appointed as the new organist and choir master. He was sorting through a number of old books and papers in the study of what was then his house but had been, in years gone by, the old precentor's house – you know, when abbeys still had secular canons. Several predecessors had left the accumulated music of bygone years and he had wanted to clear the unnecessary out-of-date material.

As he rummaged in the bookcases he came across a wider shelf than the usual. As he discarded the long undusted volumes of Victorian theology there were more books; a row of curiously incongruous older volumes set deep in the recess. The works of the Marquis de Sade, some books of necromancy, an ancient key and plan of the abbey, and, far more to his taste, some beautifully bound hand-written books with loose leaf music in them.

He still recalls the almost electric shock he felt on first opening them. As a passionate lover of that particular period of classical church music, he was ecstatic with the find. It dated from the later end of the 18th century and was the detailed structure of a series of winter choral works written by a predecessor not unknown for his flair for hymn writing. Three books in all written in careful black handwriting; two volumes covering the winter festivals, from Advent through epiphany to Quinquagesima.

The Christmas festival itself was strangely missing, but there was one special service for Sunday after Christmas; he still believes it to be the first example of the nine lessons and carols. But the carols were all quite unknown and the lessons very unusual. He looked them up. They were a strange assortment: the destruction of Aei, the witch of Endor, the Garasene Demoniac, the raising of Lazarus; but the music was exceptional. Obviously the unpublished life work of his long deceased predecessor.

There was also a journal, the third volume, written in an archaic language, difficult to decipher. He put it to one side, intending rather to transcribe just one service. With the music for the Sunday after Christmas there was a special separate part for the solo treble – very complicated, but exquisite material – and underneath the part, some writing, like that in the journal, too faded to make out. It looked like notes on where the chorister should stand, but he felt it unnecessary to decipher and put it on one side.

As the Christmas season was approaching, he was keen for some attempt to be made to resurrect this ancient lost masterpiece. He admitted to some degree of self interest in this, for to produce such a beautiful piece in his first year would make a considerable impact. He would, of course, have to change some at least of the lessons before the clergy would take to it, but that was easy. Apparently he had a bit of a struggle to get the unmusical incumbent to accept the idea but eventually he managed.

Quite remarkably the music and singing seemed to transform the choir. Even at the first attempts they began to sing as they never had before. They were all delighted with the innovation. It seemed to belong to the place, they said ... He kept quiet about where he found it, and, I believe, rather claimed it as his own work – but that's by the way.

The boy trebles were transformed and the solo was ethereal in its quality of sound – ringing into the high arches of the building with the clarity all found breathtaking, almost too much sound to emanate from one voice. But it was pure and exact in its precision. The boy's parents on hearing of their son's new excellence would come into the church and sit at the back to admire during rehearsals. They were transfixed.

Such was the excitement over the music for this particular service that the festival of Christmas began to take second place. The parents of the boy choristers and the men of the choir all concurred that the service of nine lessons and carols should be given wider recognition, and special posters and publicity were organised for it. By mid-December it was hailed as a new masterpiece by the musical authorities who had been drawn by the publicity and had come to rehearsals.

It was the beginning of the fame that was to embrace the choir and has persisted through the years of its winter festivals. Alas, the Christmas services did not go as well. From what Stevas told me, all musical effort was concentrated on what was to follow, and the incumbent was not pleased. He awaited the nine lessons and carols with scepticism. Stevas gathered that his job depended on its performance.

Two days after Christmas the boy treble's parents came to see Stevas. He greeted them with expectation of adulation. But rather they came in some aggravation. They blamed the over-excitement, the stress of the long rehearsals that had begun to last late into the nights, over-tiredness ... But the nightmares, the dreadful nightmares and fantasies – they could keep them to themselves no longer.

The boy's dream was a recurring one – of the abbey at night: a long unlit winding stairway, a small room, of cold stone walls, and a chain by a window opening. In his nightmare the boy would stretch to peer through the window – set high in the triforium above the choir stalls – and sing out from the height – sing until his lungs burst, sing the treble solos he so loved. But always the chain was set around his legs, restraining him from appearing at the window; he would sing, but he must never be seen from below.

They spoke of his sobbing in his half slumber and the contortion of his limbs wrapped round by the entangled sheets. And in the mornings, they said, his contortions remained – his limbs not working properly, his shoulders dipping as if under some terrible weight. The boy had not wanted them to come, worried that he should not be allowed to sing.

Stevas listened, with some dismay and concern – concern lest this aberration impair the success of the now highly publicised and eagerly awaited performance.

He assured them that it was nothing, that sacrifices had to be made, that, yes, the boy was probably under a strain but what possible fame was his if he persisted ... Excuses, he realised, but the thing could not be held without their son.

On seeing the boy next Stevas noted that he did wear a different air; he had begun to drag one foot, as if injured, and, the child had begun to hold his copy with a twisted hand as if suffering from some kind of crippling ailment. But it was only three days away from the performance and, even if his body was somehow deformed, the voice was as strong and as ethereal as ever.

That evening, returning home after rehearsals, something about the boy's nightmares came back to him – something about the stone room which in his dreams the boy had entered.

Stevas went to the locked cupboard in which he kept the original handwritten books. He searched through to find the place and held it carefully under his desk lamp. The rubrics describing about where the treble chorister should stand to sing the solos that were pivotal to the pieces. As he scrutinised the faded writing, a sudden movement and sound startled him; it was a heavy clunk of something falling on the floor. He started up and looked around. It was the ancient key. It had in some way become dislodged from its place in the cupboard, and both it and the plan of the abbey now lay on the floor, the map opened.

He got back to studying the writing. He couldn't make out much, only the words: '... secured as not to be seen by those below ...' and something he couldn't decipher, and then: '... to be heard but not seen is essential to the appreciation of the work ...'

How he gained access to the secret staircase he did not tell me but he found it by aid of the plan and the locked door that stood at the top. He placed the key in the lock and would have turned it, but heard a shuffling within, a scraping and whimpering sound, as if some animal moved about and the sound of chains dragging across the floor. He said he listened for some moments to the hoarse breathing and then fled down the narrow spiral ... He never ventured there again.

The night of the performance came and the boy treble was the worst he had seen him, hunched and cramped with lines of pain on his face, so much so that the boy was allowed to sit in the back of the choir stalls out of sight as the rest of the choir processed through the church; the building was thronged with people, many well known in musical if not church circles, some hundred or so having to stand at the back for lack of seats.

The festival was a resounding success, receiving acclamation from all the best newspapers the following day, setting the seal on Stevas's rise to fame. The praise for the treble solo echoed around the musical world. But the boy himself Stevas saw at the end of the performance was hunched and crippled in the back stalls. Stevas went up to him to congratulate him on his singing but was met with tears. The boy uttered only a few words; he had not been able to sing a note, he said, so horrifying were the pains in his head.

He never did sing, I believe. The doctors said it was meningitis; the child died before January was out.

Well, that's the story Stevas told me. It didn't stop him, of course. You can recognise his identity now I suppose, we haven't that many famous choirmasters in the country, and he has received recognition enough by the honours that have been heaped upon him. But the choir never toured, they always sang there and part of his mystique was always to keep the treble soloists incognito – justifiably, I should think ...

Yes, there is some kind of sequel. He told me that Christmas morning that he had burned all the original manuscripts ... and no one else has been able to get the same results from the music. That's certainly true.

The sequel? Oh yes, the sequel. A couple of years after Stevas left the abbey a new incumbent was appointed and he had some internal renovations done in the church. The Victorian pulpit was dismantled and they found an archway that had been concealed behind it. Through the archway there was a stone staircase, and at the top of this a door. The door was locked but the key was still in it. They opened the door and found the remains of a corpse chained up there. It was of a boy, or so they thought, probably about fourteen years old, but the age was hard to estimate as the corpse had been hideously deformed. It was a monster. They judged that the body had been there for a couple of hundred years. A search was made in the records and there was an account of an orphaned child of terrible appearance that had been adopted by the precentor and choir master in the late eighteenth century. Apparently the child was terrible to look at but had the voice of an angel ... Yes, you've guessed of course – there never was a boy who sang the treble solos – not one alive anyway.

Well, I told you it wasn't a nice story ... yes, I suppose it's time for bed. Sleep well.

Notes on the Contributors

A.L. Barker has published in many magazines in England, the United States, and on the Continent, as well as her seven novels and seven collections of stories. Her first book of short stories was awarded the first Somerset Maugham Prize in 1947. One of her novels was short-listed for the Booker-McConnell prize in 1969. A new novel, *The Gooseboy*, is to be published in 1987. She is a Fellow of the Royal Society of Literature, was a serving member of the Executive Committee of PEN and in 1984 was on the panel of judges for the Katherine Mansfield Prize.

Meg Buxton was born in 1926 in Thorverton, near Exeter, Devon; educated at Sherborne School for Girls and Edinburgh Art College. Lives in a very old house in Cornwall which she bought 22 years ago for peanuts, as it was falling down, and restored, mostly with her own hands. Lives with second husband, ex-Grenadier Guards officer, two Salukis, one Siamese cat, 47 fantail pigeons, two found-in-the-road budgerigars and a goldfish called Florence. Is mad about history, old buildings, architecture, animals, designing anything, plants, but most of all words and their derivations. She has published two collections of ghost stories, and contributed to several anthologies.

R. Chetwynd-Hayes has been a full-time writer since 1973 and during the ensuing period has written and published six novels, seventeen collections of short stories, edited 33 anthologies, novelised two films and had two films based on his stories. Before becoming a full-time writer he was a salesman and assistant buyer in Harrods, the Army and Navy Stores and Bourne and Hollingsworth, then showroom and exhibition manager for Peerless Built-in Furniture. During the war he was evacuated from Dunkirk and then returned to France on D-Day plus 6. During 1987 he has published two collections of short stories on the descendants of Dracula.

Kelvin I. Jones was born in Bexley, Kent, in 1948 and has always sustained a twin interest in the detective and ghost story. He is a prolific contributor to the literature about Conan Doyle and Sherlock Holmes (four full length books and countless magazine articles here and in the USA over the past twenty years). He has also written numerous short stories, drawing on his two sources of inspiration: the tradition of M.R. James and the rich folklore of England. He is married and lives in Rochester within a stone's throw of the cloisters shrouding the mystery of Edwin Drood.

Lanyon Jones is the Chaplain of Rugby School. One of his greatest enjoyments beyond his work at the school is writing, which is done in the holidays at his home in Cornwall. Among other things he writes an annual Christmas ghost story to entertain family and friends.

Brian Lumley was born on the north-east coast of England in 1937. Always a reader of macabre fiction, he was early influenced by the work of H.P. Lovecraft and 'might have started to write earlier but there was always a wanderlust in me, and the Army got to me first.' At the age of thirty while stationed in Berlin with the Royal Military Police he submitted his first real stories to August Derleth of Arkham House in the USA, and by the time he completed his military career some ten of his books were in print in America and elsewhere. Addicted to skin diving, spear fishing and hang gliding, his stories are not surprisingly usually vivid tales of high adventure set against darkly macabre and alien worlds.

Ross McKay was born in Canada in 1948, and came to live in Glasgow in 1956. He read politics and modern history, later specialising in Soviet Studies, at Glasgow University, where he was the editor of the undergraduate newspaper. Since leaving university he has worked in public relations, been a labourer, a night porter, a city councillor and a civil servant. After much wandering about, he married an Australian girl in 1981 and they have two daughters. He writes his stories in between letters of complaint to British Rail about poor services to his Cambridgeshire home.

John Marsh has been an author for many years. He has published over 100 novels under his own and several pen-names as well as a large output of short stories. Many have appeared in the USA as well as European countries. His best-known non-fiction works are *The Young Winston Churchill* and *Clip a Bright Guinea*. The first deals with the first 25 years of the statesman's life, the other the story of the Yorkshire coiners of the 18th century. The Churchill book has, since its publication in 1956, sold over 300,000 copies here and in the States.

Alma Priestley was born and brought up in Yorkshire and is a librarian and a graduate of University of London. Travelled widely as an army wife, has two grown up children, and is now living and working in Edinburgh, where her husband also works. This is her third published ghost story in Kimber collections.

Mike Sims was born in London in 1952. He is the author of numerous supernatural short stories including the collection *Shadows at Midnight* co-authored with Len Maynard. Together they have written two successful horror novels under a pseudonym.

Derek Stanford Born 1918 and brought up in a (then) rural part of Middlesex within sight of the high ground of Richmond Park. His short novella 'The Haunted Suburb' describes this background which remains important to him. After law studies and war service he lived by writing and lecturing, publishing much on the 1890s, including *Three Poets of the Rhymers' Club* (Carcanet Press) and his latest book *The Vision and Death of Aubrey Beardsley* (Radcliffe Press) 1985.

Editor, critic and poet, he seeks in his own paranormal stories to create atmospheric narrative prose-poems to express both the horror and beauty of their themes. Nine of his tales have appeared in supernatural anthologies by William Kimber.

Jean Stubbs has been writing for 25 years and in that time she has produced 16 novels and innumerable short stories, reviewed regularly for *Books and Bookmen*, frequently lectured at seminars and writers' summer schools, worked for two years for an industrial publisher, and in 1984 was writer-in-residence for Avon. Her latest novel, *A Lasting Spring*, was published in July 1987 by Macmillan. A Londoner for over 20 years, she moved to Cornwall with her second husband in 1975 and has lived there ever since in a

200-year-old cottage.

J.C. Trewin, Cornishman from The Lizard, worked for *The Morning Post* during its last years, and then for a long time on *The Observer* (including nearly six years as literary editor). The longest-serving drama critic (at present, *The Illustrated London News*, *The Lady* and *The Birmingham Post*) he has written fifty books, mainly theatrical and biographical and edited fifty others. He received the OBE in 1982 and is a Fellow of the Royal Society of Literature. He has contributed to many Kimber anthologies.

Fred Urquhart was born in Edinburgh in 1912, spent his childhood and youth in various parts of Scotland, but has lived for more than half his life in England, particularly in Sussex where he has been for over a quarter of a century. He has been a bookseller, a literary agent, a reader for Metro-Goldwyn-Mayer, London 'scout' for Walt Disney, and a reader and editor for Cassell, Hamish Hamilton, Dent and several other publishers. He has published four novels but is probably best known for his short stories, many of which have been broadcast, translated and appeared in numerous anthologies.

John Whitbourn is in his twenties, an archaeology graduate and works in Local Government. He, his wife and their baby son Joseph live in a part of south-east England where his family have resided for at least 400 years and probably longer. 'Waiting for a Bus' is part of a larger work entitled *The Binscombe Tales*, a series of supernatural stories set in a present day suburban community and all involving the enigmatic Mr Disvan and his associate, Mr Oakley. He describes them as an updating of the traditional ghost story and as an attempt to construct a mythology for modern England. He has also written several science fiction novels concerning 'alternative histories' and time travel.